How to use our guide

- All the practical information, hints and tips that you will need before and during the trip start on page 101.
- For general background, see the sections Vienna and the Viennese, p. 6, and A Brief History, p. 12.
- All the sights to see are listed between pages 22 and 72, with suggestions on excursions from Vienna from page 72 to 85.
  Our own choice of sights most highly recommended is pinpointed by the Berlitz traveller symbol.
- Entertainment, nightlife and all other leisure activities are described between pages 86 and 92, while information on restaurants and cuisine is to be found on pages 94 to 100.
- Finally, there is an index at the back of the book, pp. 126–128.

Although we make every effort to ensure the accuracy of all the information in this book, changes occur incessantly. We cannot therefore take responsibility for facts, prices, addresses and circumstances in general that are constantly subject to alteration. Our guides are updated on a regular basis as we reprint, and we are always grateful to readers who let us know of any errors, changes or serious omissions they come across.

Text: Jack Altman
Photography: Jean-Claude Vieillefond
Layout: Doris Haldemann
We wish to thank Anna Kobrak and Johanna Katzensteiner for their contribution to the preparation of this guide. We're also grateful to the Austrian National Tourist Office—particularly Johann Timko—and the Austrian Airlines for their valuable assistance.
4 Cartography: 🔵 *Falk* Falk-Verlag, Hamburg

BERLITZ®

VIENNA

1989/1990 Edition

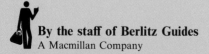

By the staff of Berlitz Guides
A Macmillan Company

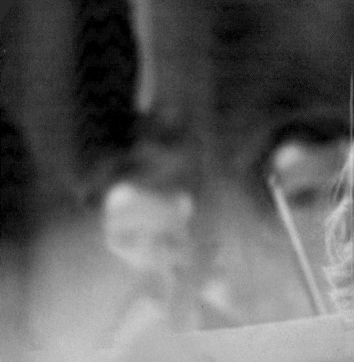

12th Printing
1989/1990 Edition

Contents

Cover picture: Schönbrunn

Vienna and the Viennese

More than most, Vienna is a city of legends. Part of the adventure of going there is discovering how much is true, how much fantasy.

Are the Viennese really so charming, witty and worldly? Are the palaces and churches as grand, elegant and graceful as they say? Do those horses at the Spanish Riding School walk on air? Do the taxi-drivers actually hum a few bars of *The Magic Flute* as they drive you to the opera? Does the Sachertorte chocolate cake melt in your

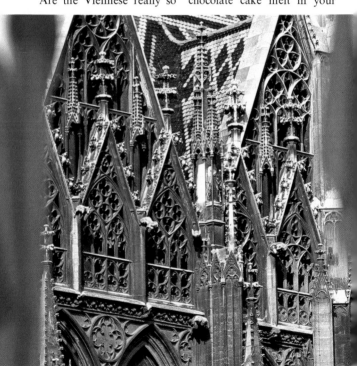

mouth? Can that violin in the Heurigen wine-garden really move a bank manager to tears?

The answer to this kind of question is of course yes. And no. Judge for yourself. The Danube, you'll notice, is brown, like any other big city river these days, but a small section of it, siphoned off

The old city's gracious traditions are chiselled on the noble façade of the Stephansdom cathedral and on the pensive faces of elderly ladies.

through the Donaupark, turns out to be as blue as the waltz promised us. Nothing in Vienna is straightforward.

Where is Vienna, for instance? East or West? According to the wily 19th-century statesman Metternich, if you go beyond the Landstrasse—a busy shopping street leading eastwards from the centre of town—you'll find yourself in the Balkans. But, as the capital of the Habsburg empire that included not only Slavs and Hungarians but also Germans, Spaniards, Italians and Belgians, Vienna has always been an outpost and gateway of Western civilization. After the opening of the Vienna International Centre, or UNO-City, in 1979, Vienna, fittingly—and officially—became one of the three U.N. cities.

A melting pot long before New York, Vienna has perpetually defied a simple national label. Its language is German—with a distinctive Viennese touch; but the city and the people obviously have too much Balkan and Latin in them to be grouped with Hamburg, Berlin or Frankfurt. The wind that sweeps down that Landstrasse has the unmistakable bite of the steppes but by the time it reaches the centre of town, as often as not, it's been tamed by a warm breeze from the south. At the foot of the lofty Stephansdom (St. Stephen's Cathedral) you feel yourself squarely in a northern, Gothic tradition. But if you go up the belltower and look west to the city's vineyards on the slopes of the Wienerwald, the dreamy panorama can persuade you it's time for a siesta.

Much of the town's 18th-century charm and 19th-century pomp have withstood the onslaught of World War II bombs, post-war building speculation and the inevitable pollution of modern traffic. Its exhilarating tree-lined Ringstrasse, encircling the Innere Stadt (Inner City), compares favourably with the airy sweep of Parisian boulevards. In every sense the heart of the city, the Innere Stadt has baroque palaces, elegant shops, gay cafés—or musty ones, depending on your taste—the illustrious Burgtheater and Staatsoper (State Opera) and the narrow medieval streets winding around the cathedral.

Outside the Ring, the city sprawls through 22 other dis-

Young people go to the Prater to let their hair down on the crazy rides at the big amusement park.

tricts with plentiful parks and even farms and vineyards inside the city limits. Vienna has space to relax, a city in a rural setting that makes the attitude to life of its 1,650,000 population more easy-going than in most modern cities of its size.

This pleasant atmosphere

Decked out in traditional bowler hat, driver of horse-drawn Fiaker waits for a customer to regale with the city's lore and legends.

always comes as a surprise to visitors. Most of the people still seem to have time for the courtesies of the old days. Shopkeepers like to call their regular customers by aristocratic titles that, constitutionally, should have disappeared 60 years ago, or at least by a nicely inflated professional title.

If ladies' hands are not kissed as often as they used to be, the intention is still announced— *"Küss die Hand, gnädige Frau"* (I kiss your hand, gracious lady)—with a gesture and a lilt in the voice that remind you Vienna has remained the city of music. Here, incidents at the opera or personnel changes at the philharmonic claim the front-page banner headlines reserved elsewhere for threats of war. Tenors, sopranos and conductors have the star-status of film actors, and the hall porter will tell you whether this year's *Don Giovanni* measures up to his favourite of a few years back. It is hard to say whether Vienna is like that because Mozart, Beethoven and Mahler chose to live here or they chose to live here because Vienna is like that.

Today the city is proud of its social progress, its strong trade unions and prosperous middle class. It has come to terms with its modest role in world events—or perhaps even feels relieved. But the past continues to haunt the Viennese consciousness, accounting for an occasional wistful but smiling melancholy. Nostalgia is a permanent Viennese trait—now some regret the passing of the Habsburgs, but 700 years ago, when the Habsburgs first ar- **11** rived, a Viennese chronicler was lamenting "the good old days" of their predecessors, the Babenbergs. Although recent social innovations by the government have been generally popular in Vienna, the people remain profoundly conservative. Not by politics so much as by instinct. Politically the Viennese have always been impossible to define. They cheered their Habsburg emperors and then Napoleon. They welcomed the republican experiment after World War I and then cheered Hitler. But that may be because the Viennese like any kind of parade.

No word better describes the ideal of Viennese life than *Gemütlichkeit*. Literally untranslatable, *gemütlich* means cozy, agreeable, comfortable. As unmistakable as a Viennese smile, it is the quality that takes the rough edges off life. And the Viennese protect the *Gemütlichkeit* of their lives with their undying ironic sense of humour. Nothing is so bad that it doesn't have a good side and nothing so good that there isn't a risk somewhere. According to an old joke, "Everything in Vienna is *gemütlich* except the wind." "Yes," goes the answer, "and the wind comes only because it's so *gemütlich* here."

A Brief History

Vienna has been busy welcoming or trying to repel foreign visitors since the beginning of recorded time. When the Romans arrived in the first century A.D., they found the place inhabited by very cooperative Celts who had come from Gaul 400 years earlier. The Roman soldiers, sent from Britain to defend the empire's eastern European frontiers, set up their garrison—Vindobona—in the middle of what is now the Innere Stadt (Inner City).

The Romans had their work cut out fending off invasions of the Teutons and Slavs, defending this crossroads on the River Danube, which linked western and eastern Europe. Emperor Marcus Aurelius personally led the fight against the barbarians and died in Vindobona in the year 180. A hundred years later, another Roman emperor, Probus, stayed long enough to introduce wine-growing on the slopes of the Wienerwald. Today, a street in the very heart of the Heurigen wine district of Heiligenstadt, Probusgasse, honours him for this initiative.

Christianity arrived some time in the 4th century and Vienna's first church was built on the present site of the Peterskirche. Inevitably, Attila the Hun turned up, in 453, but he died before implementing his plans for the conquest of Vienna. His Huns departed soon afterwards.

Others, like the Goths, Franks, Avars, Bavarians, Magyars and Slavs were more persistent and burned, plundered and pillaged their way through poor young Vienna, even in the face of Charlemagne's pacification efforts at the end of the 8th century. Then in 1156 the Babenbergs, who had succeeded a century and a half earlier in driving the Magyars out, were named hereditary dukes of Austria by the Holy Roman Emperor.

The first duke, Heinrich II Jasomirgott, set up his court around what is today the Platz am Hof. Vienna was launched into its first golden era. Art, trade and handicrafts thrived, attracting immigrant German merchants and artisans. Scottish and Irish monks on their way to Jerusalem stopped off to found a monastery—Schottenstift. The first Stephansdom was built. Vienna had become an important stopover on the way to and from the Crusades. During the 13th century many new churches, like the Michaelerkirche, went up in Vienna, as well as several monasteries, elegant residences for the nobility along the broad new thoroughfares and a fortress on the site of the future Hofburg castle. The Innere Stadt began to take on its present shape. It was also the great era of the minstrels, the start of Vienna's long musical tradition.

But it was all too good to be true. Friedrich II, known as Friedrich der Streitbare (the Belligerent), disturbed Vienna's hard-earned peace by picking fights with his barons, seducing the burghers' wives and going off to war at the slightest imagined provocation.

The Habsburgs Arrive

In 1246 the male line of the Babenbergs died out and the country fell to Ottokar II of Bohemia. Ottokar was popular with the Viennese. He made attractive additions to the Stephansdom and started on the Hofburg. So the people did not at all appreciate the efforts of the new German king Rudolf von Habsburg to gain control of the city. They supported Ottokar, but in 1278 Rudolf triumphed.

Vienna's history for centuries thereafter is by and large that of a constant confrontation between the Habsburgs' visions of grandeur and world con- **13** quest and the citizens' taste for the quiet life. Whenever the Habsburgs went about their empire-building, under Maximilian I, Karl V and Ferdinand I, Vienna was neglected. The rulers the people liked best were the ones that preferred to stay home and build things. Rudolf der Stifter (the Founder) created the university in 1365 and turned the Romanesque Stephansdom into a Gothic structure. Friedrich III completed the work and won Rome's approval for Vienna to become a bishopric in 1469—the Viennese showed their appreciation by burying him, exceptionally, in the cathedral. As his tomb attests, Friedrich was the one who dreamed up the grandiose motto: A.E.I.O.U. —"Austria Est Imperare Orbi Universo", for which an English approximation might be "Austria's empire is our universe".

Hungarian king Matthias Corvinus occupied Vienna from 1485 to 1490. He's remembered for his remark: "Let others wage war, while you, happy Austria, arrange marriages. What Mars gives to others, you receive from Venus". The reference was to the Habsburgs' knack of expanding their empire by judicious mating of their innumerable archdukes and archduchesses—a policy used to great advantage by Maximilian I.

Picking up where the Goths and the Magyars left off, the Turks under Suleiman the Magnificent staged a crippling 18-day siege of Vienna in 1529. The suburbs were devastated but the Innere Stadt held fast and the infidels were finally forced to retreat.

During the 16th century, the Reformation made considerable inroads in Vienna, but it was Catholicism that ultimately triumphed. The city emerged as a bulwark of the Church, standing not only against the Muslim Turks but also the Protestant Swedes who launched an unsuccessful attack during the Thirty Years' War.

It was Emperor Leopold I who ushered Vienna into its glorious baroque era, a feast of architecture and music that scarcely paused to deal with the vicious plague of 1679 and another Turkish siege in 1683. The great soldier and scholar Prince Eugene of Savoy came to Vienna after his campaigns for the Habsburgs. He built the magnificent Belvedere Palace, and the Schwarzenbergs, Auerspergs and Liechtensteins followed suit on a more modest but equally

Illuminated stained-glass in the 12th-century Abbey of Klosterneuburg.

elegant scale. Karl VI, pretender to the Spanish throne, returned to Vienna more Spaniard than Austrian and brought with him the strict formality and piety of the Spanish court. He redid the 12th-century Abbey Klosterneuburg in baroque style in an attempt to create an Austrian version of El Escorial. The Karlskirche, designed on a grand scale, was originally intended to emulate St. Peter's in Rome. The Hofburg underwent a magnificent expansion: the Spanish Riding School and the Imperial Library were built. Vienna began to vie with Versailles—and anticipated Napoleon with triumphal arches, torn down later when the Viennese got tired of them. **15**

Maria Theresa

After this feverish construction that crowned the efforts of the male Habsburgs, those resolute empire-builders, the Viennese were delighted to be able to relax under the maternal eye of Maria Theresa (1740–80). Pious, warm and sentimental, this mother of 16 children had an unerring feel for the moods of her capital's citizens. She was

Schönbrunn Palace park was a favourite refuge from the cares of the state for Austria's beloved ruler, Maria Theresa—and her 16 children.

an enthusiastic patron of the arts, but most of all of music. She loved to have concerts and operas performed at her newly completed Schönbrunn Palace, which she infinitely preferred to the forbidding Hofburg fortress. Her orchestra director was Christoph Gluck. Young Joseph Haydn sang in the Vienna Boys' Choir and six-year-old Wolfgang Amadeus Mozart won Maria Theresa's heart by asking for the hand of one of her daughters. (As luck would have it, the daughter in question, Marie Antoinette, was destined to lose her head for somebody else.) In the following years, these three com-

posers—Gluck, Haydn and Mozart—were to make Vienna's reputation as a city of music.

Maria Theresa lulled the Viennese into a false sense of security. Her son Joseph II (1780–90), very serious-minded and not very tactful, shocked them into a reluctant awareness of the revolutionary times that were coming. He rushed through a series of far-reaching reforms, making life easier for peasants, Protestants and Jews. But the conservative Viennese were just not ready. They were startled to see him open up the city by tearing down the wall around the Innere Stadt and impressed by the bureaucratic machine he installed to run the empire. But ultimately they felt happier with his more passive and cynical nephew, Franz II.

The French Revolution got off to a bad start in Vienna: the Republic's first envoy, Jean-Baptiste Bernadotte (later King Charles XIV of Sweden) arrived in 1798 and promptly flew the strange tricolour flag in the faces of passers-by, who tore it—and the two countries' diplomatic relations—to shreds. The Viennese were slightly less bumptious when Napoleon's armies arrived in November 1805 and the French emperor moved into Maria Theresa's beloved Schönbrunn on his way to further glories at Austerlitz.

For centuries the Habsburgs' secret weapon in foreign policy had been astute marriages—with Maria Theresa the undisputed champion. Now, when it was a question of saving what was left of the empire, Emperor Franz did not hesitate to give his daughter Marie-Louise in marriage to his enemy Napoleon in 1810. The Viennese did not protest. Anything for a quiet life.

The Congress of Vienna

The Napoleonic era ended with one of the city's most splendid moments, the Congress of Vienna, organized by Franz's crafty chancellor Metternich for the post-war carving up of Napoleon's Europe. Franz was happy to leave the diplomatic shenanigans to Metternich while he supervised a non-stop spectacle of banquets, balls and concerts—all the things the Viennese loved best. Many consider Franz was more successful than Metternich. "This Congress does not make progress", said the Belgian Prince de Ligne, "it dances".

For the next 30 years or so the city relaxed for a quiet period of good living—dubbed the *"Backhendlzeit"* (roast chicken era)—an almost democratic time, with the Prater park a favourite outing for royalty and worker alike. And it was time for more music. Beethoven had became the darling of an aristocracy eager to make amends for its shameful neglect of Mozart. But in general the taste was more for the waltzes of Johann Strauss, father and son.

In 1848, Vienna got caught up in the wave of revolution that spread across Europe in support of national independence and political reform. Ferdinand, the most sweet-natured but also most dim-witted of Habsburg emperors, exclaimed when he heard that disgruntled citizens were marching on his Hofburg: "Are they allowed to do that?" He fled town before getting an answer. Metternich was forced out of power and the mob hung the war minister Theodor Latour from a lamppost before imperial troops brutally re-established order.

Ferdinand abdicated and his deadly earnest nephew Franz Joseph took over. Grimly aware of his enormous burden, Franz Joseph concentrated throughout his 68-year reign on defending his family's interests and preserving as much of the empire as possible for as long as it could hold out. Vienna offered him a paradoxically triumphant arena in which to preside over the inevitable imperial decline. Profiting from the recent prosperity of the industrial revolution, the city enthusiastically developed the great Ringstrasse complex, with imposing residences for the new aristocracy of capitalism and residential districts for the burgeoning bourgeoisie.

The World's Fair in 1873 sang the city's praises and people travelled across Europe to see the grand new opera house, the theatres, concert halls and museums. The cultural achievements of the empire were to be consecrated in monumental form before the empire itself disappeared. Brahms, Bruckner and Mahler, Lehar and Strauss provided the music. At the Secession gallery, a group of young artists introduced a new style of art, Vienna's version of Art Nouveau, which came to be known as *Jugendstil*. Only a spoilsport like Sigmund Freud over at the university would suggest that the Viennese examine the depths of their unconscious for the seeds of their darker impulses. Little wonder they were in no mood to pay attention. In the coffee houses the intellectuals clucked disapprovingly and **19** the town waltzed on. A would-be painter named Adolf Hitler left town in disgust at this lack of seriousness, blaming the Jews and Slavs he had encountered in Vienna for the problems of the "true Germans".

The End of the Empire

Having lost his son Rudolf through a romantic suicide in Mayerling and his wife Elisabeth to an assassin's knife in Geneva, Franz Joseph was stricken but fatalistic when he heard that his heir Archduke Franz Ferdinand had been shot dead with his wife in Sarajevo. The World War (1914–18) that followed ended the Habsburg empire and left Vienna in economic and social ruin.

Vienna lost its hinterland of Czechoslovakia, Hungary, parts of Poland, Rumania and

Brahms ponders a lullaby, destined to charm his many admirers.

Yugoslavia, on which it had depended not only for its economic prosperity but also for its cultural enrichment. True, the state opera could boast Richard Strauss as its director and architecturally the old creative spirit re-emerged in the imaginative public housing, but things were not the same. The city suffered from crippling inflation and vicious street fighting between socialists and the extreme right-wing forces of the Dollfuss government.

In 1934, Austrian Nazis stormed the Ballhausplatz and assassinated Chancellor Dollfuss. His successor was able to crush the putsch but it was only a matter of time until Hitler was ready for the *Anschluss* (annexation) of Austria.

On March 13, 1938, Hitler drove triumphantly along the Mariahilferstrasse, cheered by hundreds of thousands of Viennese who saw him as their saviour from the chaos of recent years. He was seen somewhat differently by the city's 180,000 Jews. The brutality of the Viennese Nazis shocked even people who had witnessed their counterparts at work in Germany. The expulsion and extermination of the Jews left a great stain on the city and a gaping hole in the cosmopolitan culture in which the Jews had played such an important role.

But in some small measure the city's spirit survived in those war years. The Nazi Gauleiter overseeing Vienna, Joseph Bürkel, warned Goebbels it was perhaps better to let Vienna's satirical cabaret continue: "One must give more scope to Viennese humour than is usual in the rest of the Reich". What humour was left was sorely tested by the bombardments of the last year of the war, bringing heavy destruction to the Stephansdom and almost every other major city monument.

After the war, Vienna, like Berlin, was divided into four sectors, with the Innere Stadt under the joint four-power administration of the Americans, Russians, British and French. In 1955 Austria was given neutral status, celebrated in typical style with the simultaneous reopening of the Staatsoper and Burgtheater, restored from their wartime ruins. With neutrality came the quiet life after which the Viennese had always hankered, perhaps more than they really wanted. But a spectacular economic recovery has made the town a prosperous and comfortable place in which to enjoy the fruits of its long history.

What to See

So much of Vienna's history has been crammed into its Innere Stadt that you will inevitably find yourself spending by far the greater part of your visit in this Erster Bezirk, the first of the 23 districts. Although the city has an efficient but leisurely tram system, the only way to visit the area inside the Ringstrasse is on foot.

With perhaps one reservation: for a romantic introduction to the town, take a **Fiaker tour.** The Viennese have adapted the French word *fiacre* to apply both to the two-horse open carriage and to the perky drivers, elegantly turned out in bowler hat, grey velvet jacket and black-and-white check trousers *(Pepitahose).* In business since the 17th century, they'll show you the sights with a fund of amusing if often apocryphal stories that will put you in the proper mood.

Innere Stadt

It's unthinkable to start a tour of Vienna anywhere else but at the **Stephansdom.** Never was a monument more magnetic. Whichever way you choose to walk through the Innere Stadt, you seem inevitably to end up at the cathedral and it dominates any view of the city from afar. For over eight centuries, the Stephansdom has watched over Vienna—weathering city fires, Turkish cannonballs and Russian shells.

You get the best view of the cathedral from the Graben. Stop at the corner of Stock-im-

Eisen-Platz where you can take in the western façade, with its Riesentor (the main entrance), flanked by the Heidentürme, and beyond, the steeple (448 feet high) which the Viennese, with their taste for cozy diminutives, call the *alte Steffl*. It is worth looking at the steeple in the early morning and at sunset to see how much the mass and form of the spire's open stonework change with the light.

The Riesentor (Giant's Gate) got its name from a huge

Platz am Hof, where once was hung a war minister from a lamp post.

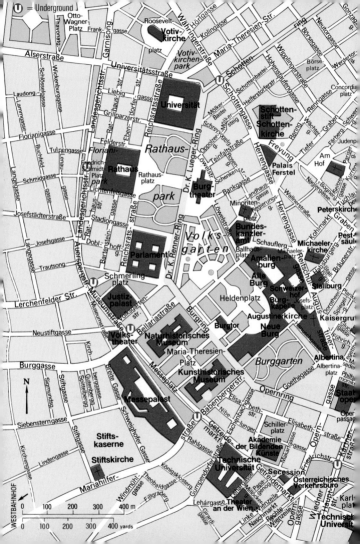

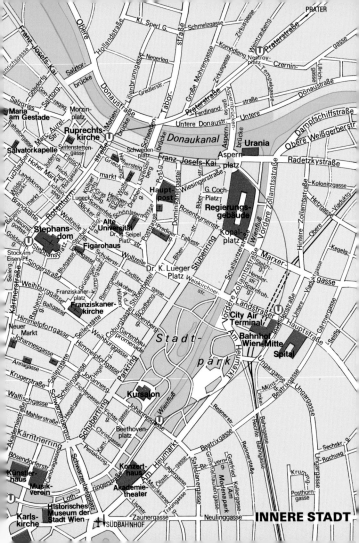

bone found during construction in the 13th century, which was thought to be the shin of a giant drowned in Noah's flood. The bone hung on the door until the Age of Enlightenment, when scientific spirits decided it was perhaps the tibia of a mammoth. The name Heidentürme (Pagan Towers) may have come from the vague resemblance to Turkish minarets.

With its Romanesque western façade, Gothic tower and baroque altars, the cathedral is a marvellous example of the Viennese genius for harmonious compromise, melding the austerity, dignity and exuberance of those great architectural styles. The Romanesque origins are visible in the Heidentürme and statuary depicting, among others, a griffin and Samson fighting a lion. Above the entrance are figures of Christ and the apostles and a veritable menagerie of dragons, lions, reptiles and birds depicting the evil spirits to be exorcized by the sanctity of the church.

Its transformation into the Gothic structure we see today was carried out mainly in the 14th and 15th centuries. To support their petition to have Vienna made a bishopric, the Habsburgs hoped to impress **26** the pope by adding a second tower to match the great south one of 1433. But the city fathers insisted the money would be better spent on strengthening the town's fortifications against the Turks and the Reformation forces. As a result, the north tower was never properly completed, just topped off in 1578 with a somewhat silly-looking Renaissance cupola. Yet part of the Stephandom's charm derives from its asymmetry, with one steeple set to the side.

From the north tower you have a fine view of the city, as well as the huge Pummerin bell cast from melted-down Turkish cannons after the 1683 siege was repelled. The present bell is a recast version of the original destroyed during World War II.

Inside the church you should look in the centre aisle for the charming carved Gothic **pulpit** by Anton Pilgram. At the head of the spiral staircase, the sculptor has placed Augustine, Gregory, Jerome and Ambrose, fathers of the Church. He also defied the customary medieval anonymity with a sculpture of himself looking

After eight centuries of wear and tear, fire and war, the Stephansdom still dominates the old city.

through a window under the staircase. No shrinking violet, Pilgram pops up again at the foot of his other contribution to the church, the elaborate stone organ-base against the wall of the north aisle.

On the left side of the high altar you'll find the carved wooden **Wiener Neustädter Altar;** on the right side is the impressive marble **tomb** of Emperor Friedrich III, honoured by the Viennese as the man who had the city made a bishopric and as the inventor of the *Semmel*, the nice little breadroll you get with every meal.

After a long visit to the cathedral you may need a coffee. Walk up the Rotenturmstrasse to one of the outdoor cafés on Lugeck, a pleasant little square where they used to hang burglars some 300 years ago. From there, wander over to the Fleischmarkt; at number 11 you'll find the **Griechenbeisl** tavern, famous for dear old Augustin, the bagpipe player who lamented the scourge of the plague around 1700 with his song: *"Ach du lieber Augustin, alles ist hin!"* (Oh dear Augustin, everything is gone!) He wasn't the only musical customer. The clients included Beethoven, Schubert, Wagner and Strauss. You'll also find **28** Turkish cannonballs embed-

ded in this last vestige of the city wall that withstood the 1529 siege.

For a sweet moment of peace go around the corner to the Grashofgasse and walk across the lovely courtyard of the 17th-century **Heiligenkreuzerhof** convent. On the other side, at the Basiliskenhaus (Schönlaterngasse 7), you'll be back in the Middle Ages of superstition. Here a basilisc—half rooster, half lizard—was said to have breathed its foul poisonous fumes into the drinking water until a baker's apprentice had the bright idea of holding up a mirror to the monster and scaring it to death. Next door was the home of composer Robert Schumann. He came from Germany to make sure the Viennese did not assign the works of Franz Schubert to oblivion.

It is a stone's throw over to the **Alte Universität** (Old University), where young Franz lived when he was a member of the Vienna Boys' Choir. The Alte Universität, founded in 1365, was closed down after the students had participated in the revolution of 1848. The authorities didn't like having these hotheads in the Innere Stadt and moved them to academies in the outer districts until a new university could be opened in 1884, safely on the outside edge of the Ring.

On the Bäckerstrasse, where the bakers have given way to antique dealers and art galleries, you can see the baroque house (No. 16) of the old Schmauswaberl restaurant which served students cheap meals with left-overs from the Hofburg kitchens. The French lady of letters Madame de Staël lived at the Palais Seilern, and across the street (at No. 7) is a beautiful ivy-covered arcaded **Renaissance courtyard,** one of the few remaining in Vienna.

Cut across the busy Wollzeile to the Domgasse, important to some as the site of Vienna's first coffee-house (see p. 99) but to most because of its association with Mozart. From 1784–1787 Wolfgang Amadeus lived in the **Figarohaus** at No. 5, now a museum devoted to the great man. In this house he wrote 11 piano concertos, 1 horn concerto, 2 quintets, 4 quartets, 3 trios, 3 piano sonatas, 2 violin sonatas and the opera *The Marriage of Figaro.* Music lovers faint at the thought that they can stand in the same room where Mozart received a respectful visit from Joseph Haydn and where the young Ludwig van Beethoven applied for music lessons. These were the great days. Four years later, a few hundred yards away in musty Rauhensteingasse, Mozart struggled to finish *The Magic Flute* and a *Requiem* before his time ran out. He died a pauper whose coffin was blessed in an anonymous ceremony for that day's dead.

Cheer yourself up with a stroll through the **Fähnrichshof** at the corner of Blutgasse and Singerstrasse. This charming complex of artists' studios, galleries, boutiques, apartments and gardens is a triumph of urban renovation after World War II bombs had left the exquisite courtyards in ruins. On your way over to the city's historically most fashionable thoroughfare, the bustling Kärntnerstrasse, stop off at the delightful little **Franziskanerplatz** to see the 18th-century fountain with a statue of Moses by Johann Martin Fischer and the ornate baroque Franziskanerkirche.

The **Kärntnerstrasse** was the city's main north-south thoroughfare, continuing on through Carinthia (Kärnten) to Trieste on the Adriatic. It has always been the central artery

On following page: *Vienna in flashes—a pretty girl, music on every corner and fine buildings like the Erzbischöfliches Palais.* **29**

of Viennese social life, perhaps because it so neatly joins the sacred and the profane—the Stephansdom at one end and the Staatsoper at the other. Many of Vienna's smartest shops can be found on the Kärntnerstrasse, as well as elegant gentlemen and grand and not so grand ladies, wandering up and down, to see and be seen in a town not noted for its street life. Today it is a traffic-free pedestrian zone with open-air cafés down the middle of the street.

Back at the Stephansdom end of Kärntnerstrasse is the **Stock-im-Eisen** (literally, stick set in iron) which provides the name for the little square leading to the Graben. The gnarled old trunk—documents first mention it in 1533—is said to be the last tree of the Wienerwald from the days when the woods bordered on this part of town. In the Middle Ages, journeymen locksmiths arriving in Vienna used to drive a nail into the trunk for good luck. The nails are still there.

The **Graben** is another fashionable shopping street, famous till the end of the Habsburg empire as a coffeehouse rendez-vous and equally infamous for the beloved "Graben nymphs", as the local ladies of the night were known. The

broad street, now a pedestrian zone, is dominated by the startling bulbous monument to the town's deliverance from the plague in 1679. The **Pestsäule** (Pillar of the Plague) is a rather bizarre mixture of humility before God and gruesome fascination with the disease itself. You'll find a much gayer celebration of faith in the **Peterskirche** (St. Peter's Church), a masterpiece by Gabriele Montani and Johann Lukas von Hildebrandt just off the Graben. The form of the building is dictated by the graceful oval of the nave, with its rows of pews curving accordingly, each decorated with three carved angels' heads. It provides a splendid example of how Viennese baroque manages more often than not to be both sumptuous and intimate.

From here you can make your way through the old **Jewish quarter,** still in large part a garment district. The Judenplatz (Jews' Square) housed a synagogue until 1421, when it was dismantled in a pogrom and its stones carted off to build an extension to the

Kärntnerstrasse has always been a good place for people-watching.

Alte Universität. Now the synagogue is in the Seitenstettengasse (No. 4), next to a weird building called the Kornhäuselturm. This was originally the studio and home of 19th-century architect Josef Kornhäusel. Inside, he built a drawbridge he could pull up when he wanted to shut himself off in his studio after a quarrel with his wife. The Judengasse leads to the city's most ancient church, the solid ivy-covered Romanesque **Ruprechtskirche,** built in the 11th or 12th century, but which probably had an 8th-century predecessor.

The Ruprechtskirche is near the north-east corner of the

original Roman settlement, Vindobona—bounded by Rotenturmstrasse on the east, Salzgries on the north, Tiefer Graben on the west, and Naglergasse and the Graben on the south. Appropriately the Marc Aurel-Strasse, named after the Roman emperor who died here in A.D. 180, takes you from the Ruprechtskirche to the **Hoher Markt** which was Vindobona's forum. A little museum (No. 2) shows the remains of two Roman houses laid bare by a 1945 bombardment. At the eastern end of the square is a gem of high Viennese kitsch, the Ankeruhr, a multi-coloured animated clock built about 1913 by a local insurance company (Charlemagne, Prince Eugène, Maria Theresa and others do their act at midday).

Go west to Salvatorgasse, past the superb Renaissance porch of the Salvatorkapelle, a happy marriage of Italian design and Austrian late-Gothic sculpture. Beyond it is the slender jewel of 14th-century Gothic, the church of **Maria am Gestade** ("Mary on the banks"—of the River Danube

that used to flow directly below it). Particularly lovely are the delicate pierced-stone tower and the canopied porch. Inside, look for the remains of Gothic stained glass in the choir.

Walk back across the Judenplatz—where with luck you may hear an open-air chamber music concert—to the spacious **Platz am Hof,** largest square of the old city. There the Babenberg dukes of Vienna, predecessors of the Habsburgs, built their fortress (on the site of

Celebrated clock on Hoher Markt features a midday parade of leading figures in the city's history.

35

No. 7) about 1150. It was strong enough to resist enemies but sufficiently pleasant and comfortable for the many festivities, tournaments and one, especially memorable, rollicking state-reception in 1165 for German Emperor Friedrich Barbarossa. The Mariensäule (column to Mary) was erected in 1667 to celebrate victory over Sweden's armies in the Thirty Years' War. In the southwest corner of the square, on a building that housed the Imperial War Ministry, is a plaque to Swiss philanthropist Henry Dunant, who founded the Red Cross after witnessing the bloody Battle of Solferino in 1859. It was on a lamp post in the middle of this square that the revolutionaries of 1848 hung the hapless War Minister Theodor Latour. And at the Am Hof church, a baroque reworking of a late-Gothic structure, the end of that strange institution, the Holy Roman Empire, was proclaimed with fanfare in 1806. Said by historians to have been neither holy nor Roman nor an empire, it was superseded by good Kaiser Franz's *gemütlich* Austrian one.

In the Bognergasse, take a look at the pretty 1907 Jugendstil façade of the Engel-Apotheke and then retreat again into medieval Vienna through narrow cobblestoned Naglergasse. This takes you to the **Freyung** triangle, flanked by the Palais Harrach (best known because Haydn's mother was

Viennese prefer fighting their wars these days on a chess board.

the family cook) and the **Schottenkirche** (Church of the Scots), founded by Scottish and Irish Benedictine monks in the 12th century.

On the south of the Freyung is the Herrengasse, the Innere Stadt's main eastbound traffic artery, blackening the baroque palaces with the perfect argument for pedestrian zones. These palaces, which belonged to the great Austrian, Hungarian, Italian and Czech families of Vienna's past—the Kinsky, the Modena, Wilczek, Pallavicini and Batthyani— now house government offices, embassies and international associations. Here, too, is

Palais Ferstel, incorporating an elegant shopping arcade, Freyung Passage, and the restored Café Central, Vienna's leading coffee house in the decades before World War I. Upstairs, a restaurant occupies the gilded premises of the old stock exchange.

Herrengasse leads right to the **Michaelerplatz** and the Hofburg (see p. 42). On the opposite side of the square, Michaelerkirche is a curious combination of styles, from late-Romanesque to baroque. Also on Michaelerplatz (No. 5) is the architecturally revolutionary **Loos-Haus.** Built by Adolf Loos, a forerunner of the German Bauhaus movement, its austere, functional use of fine materials shocked many in 1910. In fact, poor Franz Joseph refused to use the Hofburg's Michaelertor exit so that he would not have to look at the modern monstrosity.

Ring

Before tackling the Hofburg, it's a good idea to go around the Ring, probably the greatest single urban achievement of Franz Joseph. This boulevard encircling the Innere Stadt was mapped out in the 1860s along the ramparts Joseph II had begun clearing 80 years before. The project captured perfectly the energetic optimism of the times. The neo-classical buildings bring together all the great architectural styles in a celebration of the Industrial Revolution's seemingly boundless potential. A tram-ride is a good way to get the feel of the whole thing. While you can't help admiring the panache of the Ringstrasse and its imposing edifices—these are not buildings, but edifices—you may have some reservations about all the wasted space.

Start your walk at the west end of the Schottenring, in front of the Votivkirche, a neo-Gothic church built after Franz Joseph survived an assassination attempt in 1853. Next to it are the university and Rathaus (Town Hall) with a pleasant park, but proceed along the Innere Stadt side, past the impressive **Burgtheater** (see p. 89), a high temple of German theatre. Beyond the theatre is the lovely **Volksgarten.** Its cafés and concerts carry on a tradition that began with the café music of the Strauss family.

Opposite, you can by-pass the huge Parlament, built by Theophil Hansen after a long stay in Athens, and can save the Naturhistorisches and Kunsthistorisches Museum and the

Neue Burg till later (see pp. 65 and 47). The **Burggarten,** the park of Hofburg, leads to the **Staatsoper** (State Opera). It's worth taking a guided tour here before attending a perform-ance (see p. 86). The original opera house, inaugurated in 1869, was greeted with a rain of vicious criticism that drove one of the architects, Edward van der Nüll, to suicide. It was almost completely destroyed in 1945 bombardments. The new house is very much in the neo-classical spirit of the original;

Karlskirche, an imposing baroque edifice in a very human setting.

clearly the architects didn't want to risk the perils of trying to foist a new-fangled design on tradition-conscious Viennese opera lovers.

On Karlsplatz, not far from the opera house, stands the huge **Karlskirche,** undoubtedly the most important of the city's baroque churches. It was built by J.B. Fischer von Erlach for Karl VI in fulfilment of an oath made by the emperor during the plague of 1713. If possible, go at sunset for a quite awesome view of the big dome across the Karlsplatz. With its Greek temple-like façade, the Roman-style triumphal pillars topped by small Turkish-inspired towers and a dome reminiscent of Rome's St. Peter, the church embodies the universal character of the old Habsburg empire.

The church's visual impact has been somewhat diminished since the building of the Ringstrasse. However, the cool sober interior remains unchanged, with a subdued marble decor and a spacious but gentle oval ground-plan similar to that of the Peterskirche (see p. 32). The oval dome's splendid ceiling **frescoes** are by Johann Michael Rottmayr, the trompe-l'œil by Gaetano Fanti. Take a look also at the lovely painting of **St. Elisabeth** by Daniel Gran in the main chapel on the right.

In front of the church, a massive Henry Moore sculpture in a reflector pool provides a striking contrast. Also on the Karlsplatz is the fanciful **Stadtbahnpavillon** (Municipal Railway Pavilion) with its graceful green, gold and white motif of sunflowers and tulips. Newly restored, it was originally designed by Otto Wagner, who at the turn of the century led Viennese architecture away from its pompous academic tradition through the decorative Jugendstil and into functional modernism.

The temple of the Jugendstil movement can be seen back across the Wiedner Hauptstrasse at the corner of Friedrichstrasse. This is the celebrated **Secession** building (1897–98), conceived by Wagner's student Joseph Olbrich, for exhibiting the artists who broke away from the conservative academies. The gilded iron dome of laurel leaves is intended to symbolize the interdependence of art and nature in opposition to the artificial philosophy of the academy.

Jugendstil decor on the Stadtbahnpavillon. Summer concert in front of the town hall on Rathausplatz.

Palaces

Though the Habsburgs are long gone, Vienna remains an imperial city—an aura enhanced by its palaces. The most imposing is of course the **Hofburg,** home of Austria's rulers since the 13th century. It covers the south-west corner of the Innere Stadt in a hopelessly untidy but awe-inspiring sprawl reminiscent of the empire itself. Form, as they say, follows function.

The vast complex of buildings went through five major stages of construction over six centuries, and at the end there was still a big chunk unfinished. To follow the course of its de-

velopment, start right in the middle at the **Schweizerhof,** named after the Swiss Guard that used to be housed there. Here King Ottokar of Bohemia built a fortress in 1275–76 to defend himself against Rudolf von Habsburg. He wasn't successful and the Habsburgs moved in; they strengthened

the fortifications because of the unruly Viennese outside. By the Schweizertor archway you can still see the pulleys through which the chains of the drawbridge passed. But Rudolf's son, Albrecht I, didn't feel safe here and escaped to Leopoldsberg in the Vienna woods. For the next 250 years the fortress was used only for meetings with visiting kings and other ceremonial occasions. The **Burgkapelle** (Castle Chapel), tucked away in the northern corner of the Schweizerhof, was built in 1449. Originally Gothic, it was redone in baroque style and then partially restored to its original form in 1802. The Wiener Sängerknaben (Vienna Boys' Choir) sing Mass here every Sunday morning except in July, August and September.

In 1533, having defeated the Turks four years previously, Ferdinand I felt safe enough to settle in the Hofburg, bringing his barons and bureaucrats to make their homes in the nearby Herrengasse and Wallnerstrasse. Between 1558 and 1565 Ferdinand built the **Stallburg** (outside the main Hofburg complex on the north-east side

Opulent fountains and monuments punctuate the streets of Vienna. **43**

of Reitschulgasse) as a home for his son Archduke Maximilian. It was subsequently turned into stables for the horses of the Spanish Riding School on the other side of the street. The Stallburg, with its fine three-storey arcaded courtyard, is the most important Renaissance building in Vienna. Part of it is today the home of the Neue Galerie, devoted to 19th and 20th-century European art (see p. 69).

Still in Renaissance style is Rudolf II's **Amalienburg,** built between 1575 and 1611 mostly by Italian architect Pietro Ferrabosco. It has a very pleasant trapezoid-shaped courtyard. Maria Theresa redecorated it as part of her futile effort to make the Hofburg into a cozy home, and Elisabeth, wife of Franz Joseph, lived here, when she was in Vienna.

For a while the Habsburgs neglected Vienna in favour of Prague but in the 17th century they returned and tried to make the Hofburg into a kind of Versailles. Leopold I launched the city's baroque era with his **Leopoldinischer Trakt** (Leopold Wing)—a residence in keeping with the Habsburgs' new role as a world power. (Today the Leopoldinischer Trakt houses the Austrian presidency, a strictly honorary post.) Karl VI carried

the Habsburgs' new self-confidence proudly forward with the **Reichskanzlei** (Imperial Chancellory), where Franz Joseph was later to have his apartments, the Hofbibliothek (Court—now National—Library) and the Winterreitschule (Winter—better known as the Spanish—Riding School).

It was no longer necessary to call on foreign talent. Johann Bernhard Fischer von Erlach, his son Joseph Emmanuel and Johann Lukas von Hildebrandt

were among the outstanding court architects of the time. The Fischer von Erlachs (who designed the National Library) and Jean-Nicolas Jadot (responsible for the adjoining Grosser and Kleiner Redoutensaal) have made the **Josefsplatz** a marvellously harmonious baroque square. Inside the old library, a great oval hall with frescoes and walnut shelves, called the **Prunksaal,** is one of the most beautiful workrooms in the world.

The Hofburg reflects the pomp and glory of the Habsburgs' greatness.

Just off the Josefsplatz is the church that the Habsburgs favoured for their great events, the **Augustinerkirche.** The façade of this Gothic and baroque structure matches the library and Redoutensaal. Here Maria Theresa married François of Lorraine in 1736, Marie-Louise married Napoleon (in absentia) in 1810, **45** and Franz Joseph married Elisabeth in 1854. The Augustinerkirche masses rank among the finest, musically, in the city.

On the other hand, the church the Habsburgs chose to be buried in, the Kapuzinerkirche, lies outside of the Hofburg. Its **Kaisergruft** (imperial vault) contains about 140 assorted Habsburgs—emperors, empresses, archdukes and less exalted members of the family.

Even if the **Spanish Riding School** *(Spanische Reitschule)* had not claimed the world's attention for the prowess of the Lipizzaner horses, it would be worth seeing for the gleaming, quiet majesty of its white galleries supported on 46 columns. But the horses are there to be seen (except in January, February, July or August). Do book well in advance for this is the city's most popular show. The Lipizzaner, originally a Spanish breed, were raised at Lipica in Yugoslavia, not far from Trieste; since 1920 the tradition has been carried on in the Styrian town of Piber. Using methods that have not changed since the 17th century, the horses are trained to walk and dance with a delicacy that many ballet-dancers might envy. Their accomplishments include classical figures performed to the music of the polka, gavotte, quadrille and —this is Vienna, after all—the waltz. Nothing can take you further away from the 20th century than the sight of these shining white horses with gold ribbons tied into their plaited manes and tails, led in by equerries wearing cocked hats, brown tail-coats edged with black silk, white buckskin breeches, sabres and riding boots. Custom demands that gentlemen take their hats off when the equerries enter. The spectacle more than merits the gesture.

Under Franz Joseph, the Hofburg grew even bigger and threatened to burst across the Ring. At one end, the Michaelerplatz wing was completed. Meanwhile at the other end, in keeping with the ambitious ideas surrounding the Ringstrasse development in the last part of the 19th century, Franz Joseph (at the prompting of architect Gottfried Semper) embarked on a gigantic Kaiserforum (Emperor Forum). This was to have embraced the vast **Heldenplatz** (Heroes' Square) with two crescent-shaped arms, the whole extending through triumphal arches to the Naturhistorisches and Kunsthistorisches Museum. Only the first of the two crescents, the

Neue Burg could be undertaken before the empire collapsed. Today it houses a congress centre, several museums and reading rooms for the National Library (open to all on day passes). The Hofburg, like the empire, had bitten off more than it could chew.

For an idea of the human scale of what turned into the Habsburgs' folly, you should take the 45-minute guided tour of the **imperial apartments** *(Kaiserappartements)*, entrance on Michaelerplatz. With ingratiating humour, the guide will show you the splendid Gobelin tapestries; the smoking-room for the emperor's fellow officers; the enormous rococo stoves needed to heat the place; a chandelier weighing half a ton with 85 lights among the crystal; Franz Joseph's austere, no-frills bedroom with its

These Lipizzaner horses perform at the Spanish Riding School with the poetic precision of ballet dancers.

iron military cot and a water jug and basin with his double-eagle coat of arms on it; and Elisabeth's rooms and gymnasium in which she did daily exercises on wall-bars and climbing ropes to keep her wasp-waisted figure.

When you leave the Hofburg, take the Schauflergasse to **Ballhausplatz** to see the elegant 18th-century residence of the Austrian chancellors. In the time of Metternich, the world would ask what "the Ballhaus" would do next just as today it wonders about the thinking of the White House or the Kremlin. Chancellor Dollfuss was assassinated here in July 1934.

The affairs of the government were not something Maria Theresa ran away from, but she did prefer to handle them in a setting that was more *gemütlich:* **Schönbrunn** (accessible by tram and underground). As soon as she was settled on the throne in 1740, she moved into the palace that Leopold I had started for a summer residence and her father, Karl VI, had used for pheasant hunts.

If the Hofburg is the oversize expression of a dynasty that

Austria's royal family was always happy to share with the Viennese the serene beauties of Schönbrunn.

outgrew its own virility, Schönbrunn is the smiling, serene expression of the personality of one woman. J.B. Fischer von Erlach wanted to build a "Super-Versailles", but Leopold said no. The architect's next proposal was still too pompous for Maria Theresa's taste, so she brought in her favourite architect, Nikolaus Pacassi, who transformed Schönbrunn into an imposing edifice with warm and winning rococo interiors—a symbol of Maria Theresa's "idyllic absolutism".

To appreciate the emphasis that Schönbrunn puts on pleasure, rather than imperial pomp, it is best to visit the **gardens** first. Except for the Kammergarten (Chamber Garden) and Kronprinzengarten (Crown Prince Garden) to the immediate left and right of the palace, the park has always been open to the public. Maria Theresa liked to have her Viennese around her. The park, laid out in the classical French manner, is dominated by the **Gloriette,** a neo-classical colonnade perched on the crest of a hill. It is difficult to say which view is prettier—the graceful silhouette of the Gloriette

The Habsburgs liked the simple life—with a little touch of luxury. **51**

against a sunset viewed from the palace or a bright morning view from the Gloriette over the whole of Vienna to the north and the Wienerwald to the south. On the way to the Gloriette you will pass the Neptune Fountain and countless other statues of ancient mythology. East of the Neptune Fountain are the incredible **"Roman ruins"**, actually built in 1778—a half-buried "Roman palace" with bits of Corinthian columns, friezes and archways. With that Viennese knack of not taking things too seriously, this potentially ridiculous curiosity has great charm. Nearby is the Schöner Brunnen (Beautiful Spring), discovered by Emperor Matthias around 1615, from which the palace got its name. West of Neptune is a little zoo, a favourite project of Maria Theresa's husband François of Lorraine, and a Tyrolean Garden with a café and cottages.

On your way across the courtyard to the front entrance of the palace you will see on the right the Schlosstheater, now the site of summer chamber opera performances. In 1908, Franz Joseph's 60th anniversary as emperor was celebrated there with a ballet that included 43 Habsburg archdukes and archduchesses aged 3 to 18.

A guided tour of the **palace** (in English) will give you a glimpse of the sumptuous coziness in which Maria Theresa and her successors handled the affairs of state: her breakfast room, decorated with the needlework of the empress and her myriad daughters; the **Spiegelsaal** (Hall of Mirrors) in which the young Mozart gave his first royal recital; the **Chinesisches Rundkabinett** (Chinese Round Room), superbly adorned with lacquered Oriental panels, and also known as Maria Theresa's Konspirationstafelstube (roughly translatable as "top secret dining-room"). When she met here for secret consultations, a table rose from the floor with a completely prepared dinner so that no servants would be present during the conversation. You can also see the billiard room in which guests could amuse themselves while awaiting an audience with Franz Joseph (he also preferred Schönbrunn to the Hofburg and kept his mistress, actress Katharina Schratt, in a villa in the neighbouring district of Hietzing); and the bedroom in which he died—in another stiff iron bed—at the age of 86. You should not miss what is now known as the **Napoleon Room** (though it once was Maria Theresa's bedroom), where the emperor stayed on his way to the battle of Austerlitz and where his son, the Duke of Reichstadt, spent his last sad years. It is a moment both pathetic and awe-inspiring to sense Napoleon's presence in the room that now contains the death-mask and stuffed pet bird of his son.

The quite dazzling luxury of the ballrooms and dining rooms—where the last Habsburg abdicated, where Khrushchev and Kennedy met—side by side with the intimacy of the living quarters present a constant contrast of the stately and the human in the lives of the Habsburgs.

In the adjoining **Wagenburg** museum, you can marvel at a collection of coaches used by the imperial court.

Of all the palaces built by the princes, dukes and barons serving the Habsburgs, the most splendid is certainly the **Belvedere** of Prince Eugene of Savoy. Regarded by many as Vienna's finest flowering of baroque residential architecture, it rivals Schönbrunn and Hofburg.

Though close to the Innere Stadt, in the 3rd District, the palace is an enchanted world apart with its mythical sculptures, fountains, waterfalls, ponds and gardens. The **Unteres** (or Lower) **Belvedere,**
built by Johann Lukas von Hildebrandt in 1714–16, was Prince Eugene's summer home. (His winter palace is another jewel now brightening the lives of bureaucrats in the Finance Ministry on Himmelpfortgasse.) Today the Unteres Belvedere and its **Orangerie** together house the admirable collections of Austrian medieval and baroque art (see p. 68).

In the **Oberes** (or Upper)

Belvedere, completed in 1723, the prince held his banquets and other festivities. John Foster Dulles, Vyacheslav Molotov, Harold Macmillan, Antoine Pinay and Leopold Figl met there in 1955 to sign the treaty which gave Austria its independence as a neutral country. Now a museum for Austrian art (see p. 68), the Belvedere remains an essential stopping-place in your Vienna pilgrimage—even if you are not in the mood for art collections.

Nowhere will you get a more delightful view of the city skyline than from the **terrace** of the Oberes Belvedere—amazingly little changed since Bellotto-Canaletto painted it in 1760 (see p. 67). And on that terrace you will see the marvellous sphinxes, each with a different smile, impish, whimsical, sardonic, the very essence of Viennese womanhood.

To enjoy the fairytale pleasures of the main gardens start at the Oberes Belvedere

(entrance Prinz-Eugen-Strasse 27); it's easier to walk down to the Unteres than vice-versa. Best of all, go in the late afternoon to enjoy the view of the Oberes Belvedere at sunset, a picture of serene elegance. (On fine summer evenings there is a spectacular Sound and Light show.)

The Belvedere, ever a charmed haven for peace and contemplation.

The Other Vienna

Beyond the Innere Stadt and outside the Habsburg world of the Hofburg and Schönbrunn, there is another Vienna, the people's Vienna. Your first glimpse of it may be along the car or tram route between the two palaces on the Mariahilfer-strasse, the city's most popular shopping street, or en route to Vienna's most whimsical attraction, **Hundertwasserhaus.** This public housing complex in Kegelgasse was designed by Austria's best-known living artist, Friedensreich Hundert-wasser. Bright paintwork, an onion dome and other fanciful details endear the building to residents—and to the crowds of sightseers who have put this new Vienna landmark (1985) on the tourist map. You'll find it again when you go in search of the fabled **Danube.**

You're likely to see the Danube's canal before the river itself, which was diverted to the north-east in 1875. Until then, the Danube had rushed around the northern part of the Innere Stadt, often flooding residential districts after the winter thaw. Old lithographs show Habsburg archdukes travelling around the streets of Leopold-stadt by boat, delivering food and clothing to the populace.

Cross the Danube Canal at the junction of Franz-Josefs-Kai and Stubenring over the Aspernbrücke. This takes you to the **Prater** park, Vienna's own non-stop carnival (also accessible by underground U-1). If the Stephansdom had not already become the undisputed symbol of the city, the Prater's **Riesenrad** (giant Ferris wheel) built in 1897 would certainly have laid a claim—especially after the famous ride of Orson Welles and Joseph Cotten in Sir Carol Reed's film *The Third Man.* In fact, both monuments play big roles as expressions of the city's dignity and taste for fun.

The Riesenrad, with its 14 bright red cabins taking you up for a constantly changing perspective of the city's skyline, is only part of the fair that includes roller-coasters, discos, shooting ranges, restaurants and beer halls. In the good old days, as they never stop saying, the Prater cafés were serenaded by the ubiquitous Strauss family and their arch-rival Joseph Lanner (see p. 89). Originally reserved for the aristocracy for hunting and horse-riding, the Prater was thrown open to all Viennese under Joseph II, good liberal that he was. High and low mingled on warm evenings and Sunday afternoons—the

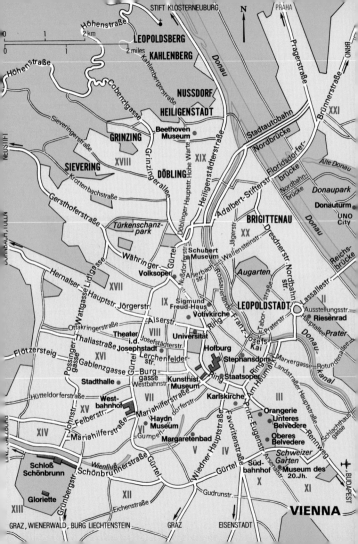

high, admittedly, still on horseback. In 1815 Czar Alexander I, Friedrich Wilhelm of Prussia, Britain's Prime Minister Castlereagh and France's Foreign Minister Talleyrand took time off for a casual parade through the Prater, dazzling the bourgeoisie along the Hauptallee.

You'll finally reach the real River Danube along the Lassallestrasse and over the Reichsbrücke. No doubt, you'll be disappointed to see that the water is a nasty yellowish brown. But this section of the river has always been like that because of the lime-content on the riverbed. Be patient and continue on the Wagramerstrasse —past the attractive modern complex of three-sided concave-curved buildings forming the United Nations City (guided tours weekdays)—to the **Alte Donau** (Old Danube). That, especially on a sunny day, is as blue as blue can be, a self-contained arm of the river closed off for sailing,

fishing and bathing. In the heart of the working-class 21st and 22nd Districts, the banks are lined with beaches, marinas and neat little gardens.

The **Donaupark** linking the old and new Danube is more tranquil than the Prater, laid out with beautiful flower beds, an artificial lake, sports arenas and a chair-lift from which to survey it all. It also features an 827-foot tower, **Donauturm,** with two revolving restaurants and a public terrace featuring a view across the city south to the hills of the Wienerwald and north-west to the Abbey of Klosterneuburg (see p. 64).

You must devote a day or two to the 19th District, **Döbling,** without a doubt the most gracious of Vienna's neighbourhoods. Stretching from the Danube Canal to the slopes of the Wienerwald, Döbling includes Sievering,

Riesenrad, giant Ferris wheel, symbolizes Vienna's high spirits.

Grinzing, Heiligenstadt, Nussdorf and Kahlenberg. It has elegant villas, parks, vineyards and, of course, the ever popular Heurigen wine-gardens (see p. 98).

If you don't have a car, start your tour by taking the tram that stops in front of the Votivkirche in Schottentor to **Heiligenstadt,** the heart of Vienna's "Beethoven country". You may want to stop off en route at the **Villa Wertheimstein** (Döblinger Hauptstrasse 96), a masterpiece of 19th-century Biedermeier architecture and furniture. At the end of the line (Heiligenstädter Park), walk across the park past a fine monument to Beethoven to Pfarrplatz 2, the prettiest of the composer's many Vienna homes.

Heiligenstadt and the other neighbourhoods of Döbling provide a vital clue to the secret of Vienna's charm. In the end Vienna is not a conventional Big City but rather a collection of villages clustered around the Innere Stadt, a source of instant relief from what the Viennese call the *Hektik* of metropolitan life.

This feeling is reinforced if you take your car (or the 38S bus from Grinzinger Allee) up to the **Höhenstrasse** to Kahlenberg and Leopoldsberg on the

Ludwig van Beethoven
(Bonn 1770–1827 Vienna)
Beethoven came to Vienna at the age of 22 to take lessons with Haydn. He soon had made quite a reputation for himself with his early piano trios and sonatas, and the Viennese aristocracy were quick to take this new genius into their homes.

These were his happiest years in Vienna. He fell in love with one after the other of the three Brunswick daughters. He wrote his "Pathétique" and "Moonlight" sonatas.

But by 1800, deafness had set in. He moved to Heiligenstadt to be near the park's reputed waters in the desperate hope that he might find a cure. It was at Probusgasse 6, in 1802, that he wrote in his famous Heiligenstädter Testament: "You are unjust, you who believe me hostile, obstinate and a misanthrope, or at least said I was. In fact you didn't know the secret reasons for the character traits you attributed to me. But could I tell you: 'Speak louder, shout, I am deaf'?"

And yet less than a year after writing that, he finished his Second Symphony, as joyous a work as any he ever wrote.

At the end of a hot afternoon try visiting a Heurigen in Grinzing.

northern slopes of the Wiener-wald. The route offers a breath-taking view of the city and surrounding countryside in a rarefied atmosphere of forest and meadow that makes it difficult to believe you are still inside the city limits. Get out and walk. The road has several inns and cafés in which to take a rest.

Since the end of the 18th century, the heights of **Kahlenberg** have been dotted with fashionable summer homes, offering what is known as *Sommerfrische* (cool summer respite from the city heat). During two steaming hot days of July 1809, the Viennese aristocracy had a grandstand view of Napoleon's Battle of Wagram against the Austrians. Sipping cool Nussdorfer white wine, they watched the manoeuvring of 300,000 soldiers on the far side of the Danube and the slaughter of 40,000 Austrians and 34,000 Frenchmen.

The Höhenstrasse goes as far as **Leopoldsberg,** the very edge of the Wienerwald and the extreme eastern point of the European Alps. On a clear day, you can see about 60 miles eastwards from the terrace of the **Leopoldskirche**

to the Carpathian mountains of Czechoslovakia.

A short detour to the north (7 km.) takes in the imposing Augustine Abbey of **Klosterneuburg.** An apocryphal story claims it was founded by Duke Leopold III of Babenberg in 1106 on the spot where the lost veil of his bride was discovered by his hunting dogs. In fact its foundation is earlier, but little of the original edifice remains. Karl VI, who was very much taken with Spain, undertook expansive—and expensive—alterations in the 18th century, making it a baroque version of the Escorial. He wanted a combination palace-church with nine domes, each topped with a crown of the House of Habsburg. Only two were completed in his lifetime: the crown of the empire on the big dome and of the Austrian archduchy on the little one. And Maria Theresa didn't have either the desire or the money to carry on.

The baroque ornamentation is impressive but the whole trip is made worthwhile by the **Leopoldskapelle** with the magnificent **Verdun Altar** of 1181, containing 45 enamelled panels depicting scenes from the scriptures. Known as a *biblia pauperum*, it was a graphic bible for the poor who could not read the stories.

Preceding page: *Heiligenstadt—where Beethoven found both musical inspiration and tranquillity.*

Museums

Kunsthistorisches Museum

If Vienna's national gallery of art is less well known than the Louvre or the Prado, it may be just because the name isn't catchy enough. For the collection is, quite simply, magnificent. Perhaps because it has benefited from the cultural diversity of the Habsburg empire, it encompasses a broader spectrum of Western European art than the more celebrated museums.

Since you can't hope to do justice to the enormous variety of the collection on a first visit, concentrate instead on a few of the outstanding works. Start with the paintings, on the first floor—Dutch, Flemish, German and English to the left and Italian, Spanish and French to the right.

Pieter Brueghel the Elder. The richness of the collection, comprising nearly half of the 15th-century Flemish artist's total output, leaves you to choose your own favourite: popular peasant themes such as *Children's Games* and *Peasant Wedding,* or biblical subjects such as *Christ Carrying the Cross* and *Building the Tower of Babel.*

Albrecht Dürer. The great German master brings the same dignity to his worldly portrait of Emperior Maximilian as to his intensely spiritual *The Holy Trinity Surrounded by All Saints.*

Lucas Cranach the Elder. An incredibly serene Judith holds the head of the Assyrian general Holophernes, which she has just cut off.

Hans Holbein. Look for the famous tight-lipped portrait of Henry VIII's third wife Jane Seymour. She, at least, died in her bed.

Anthony Van Dyck. Don't miss the dramatic, beardless *Young Field Commander.*

Peter Paul Rubens. In the extensive Rubens selection, no picture is more enjoyable than the portrait of his fat and sassy second wife Hélène Fourment—coyly titled *The Little Fur Coat.* See also Rubens' self-portrait.

Rembrandt. There are two superb paintings: the large self-portrait and the loving look at his old mother.

Jan Vermeer. *Allegory of Painting* shows the artist painting a shy young lady at the window—a familiar classic that is a pleasure to discover in the original.

Thomas Gainsborough. The evocative *Suffolk Landscape* is enough to make an Englishman homesick—and make the others understand why.

Jacob van Ruisdael. *Big Forest* serves as a soothing finale to the museum's Northern European paintings.

Titian. Vienna has a rich collection of Titians, including the majestic *Ecce Homo* of Christ before Pontius Pilate, and two lovely madonnas.

Giorgione. There are just not enough authenticated Giorgiones around to pass up the chance of seeing his *Three Philosophers.*

Tintoretto. His *Susanna in her Bath* is a delightfully wistful woman. One wonders whether she is worried by the old gentlemen watching from the sidelines.

Veronese. Never did the Bible seem more sophisticated than in this *Healing of the Haemophiliac,* by the most elegant of the 16th-century Venetian painters.

Raphael. Inspired by Leonardo, *Madonna amid Greenery* is a High Renaissance masterpiece of harmonious composition, the pyramid of Mary, Jesus and John—totally charming.

Caravaggio. There's great vigour and immediacy in his *Rosary Madonna* and *David with Goliath's Head.*

Tiepolo. Magnificent treatments of Roman history in *The Death of Brutus* and *Hannibal Recognizes the Head of his Brother.*

Velazquez. The choice is superb, second only to Madrid itself, including here the splendid *Infanta Margarita Teresa* in her blue dress and *King*

Begin the feast of Pieter Brueghel with this famous Peasant Wedding.

Philip IV and *Queen Isabella*.

Bellotto. The artist followed his uncle Canaletto's example—he even used the same name at times, producing panoramic views for the great courts of Europe. Those of Vienna include the Freyung, Neue Markt and the *City Seen from the Belvedere*.

David. At last a Frenchman. Vienna has one of the few great Davids outside the Louvre, the celebrated painting of *Napoleon Crossing the St. Bernard Pass*.

No matter how tired you might be, you should still go to see two masterworks in the groundfloor sculpture collections: **Benvenuto Cellini's** amazing gold-enamelled saltcellar for King François I of France, and the exquisite **Gemma Augustea** onyx cameo, probably first century A.D., of Augustus welcoming home his son Tiberius after defeating the barbarians of Pannonia, better known today as Austria.

Other Museums

Perhaps the Kunsthistorisches Museum manages to achieve such a balanced presentation of European art because Austrian art is housed separately at the Belvedere.

You'll find the Museum Mittelalterlicher Österreichischer Kunst (Medieval Austrian Art) in the Orangerie, the Österreichisches Barockmuseum (Austrian Baroque Museum) in the Unteres (Lower) Belvedere, and Österreichische Galerie des 19. und 20. Jahrhunderts (Austrian Gallery of the 19th and 20th Century) in the Oberes (Upper) Belvedere.

The **medieval museum** (access through the baroque gallery) has excellent examples of 15th-century statuary and altar-pieces from the Tyrol, Salzburg, Lower Austria and Styria.

The **baroque museum** presents the colourful epitome of 18th-century Vienna with warm portraits of Maria Theresa and her husband François of Lorraine. But the masterpiece of the collection is Balthasar Permoser's **Apotheosis** sculpture of Prince Eugene in the Hall of Mirrors. It shows Eugene as Hercules spurning Envy and trying to silence Fame's trumpet. The prince himself commissioned the work.

The **19th- and 20th-Century Gallery** clearly sums up Austria's image as a declining world power. On the ground floor, three rooms show the neo-classical world of the late 18th century dissolving into the plain and simple, not to say thoroughly *gemütlich* Biedermeier life of the first half of the 19th century, Vienna's *"Backhendlzeit"*. The ever-growing, self-satisfied prosperity of the times can be seen on the first floor of the gallery in the pompous and over-opulent academic style of the court favourite Hans Makart. Typically, he tried to enrich his colours by adding an alabaster base to the paint and succeeded only in causing the tones, especially the reds, to fade and crumble. Artistically more satisfying is the treatment of the same kind of imperially approved themes by

Anton Romako in his battle pictures of Admiral Tegetthoff and, again, Prince Eugene.

The second floor has a magnificent collection of the artists who captured the last glows and pain of imperial Vienna. Look for Gustav Klimt's *The Kiss* and a splendid study of the city's great bourgeoisie in his portrait of *Frau Bloch.* Vienna's new proletariat found its painter in Egon Schiele, especially in his anguished and poignant *The Family, The Artist's Wife* and *Death and the Maiden.* You can also see the fine early work of Oskar Kokoschka, his lyrical but profoundly psychological portraits.

The **Museum der Modernen Kunst** (in the Palais Liechtenstein at Fürstengasse 1) displays paintings by Marcel Duchamp, Matisse, Kandinsky, Kokoschka, Klee, Klimt, Schiele and sculptures by Giacometti and Henry Moore—in a town that still resists modern art.

Yet another art gallery worth visiting is the **Gemäldegalerie der Akademie der Bildenden Künste** (Schillerplatz 3). Highlights include *The Last Judgement* by Hieronymus Bosch and a Venetian series by Guardi.

One of the city's proudest art treasures is the **Albertina,** the world-famous collection of drawings housed at the south end of the Hofburg. Named after Maria Theresa's son-in-law, Duke Albert of Sachsen-Teschen, it was founded in 1781 and now holds nearly 40,000 original drawings and more than one million prints. The collection ranges from 15th-century Dutch, German and Italian masters through Albrecht Dürer, Leonardo da Vinci, Michelangelo, Raphael, Titian, Rembrandt, Rubens to Van Gogh, Toulouse-Lautrec, Aubrey Beardsley, and George Grosz.

Since it is obviously impossible to display all the treasures at once—and given the often fragile condition of the originals—the drawings are exhibited in special shows, changing some six times a year, each devoted to a particular period, style or theme. Any of the drawings may be seen on request.

On the other side of the street, the **Neue Galerie** (in the Stallburg at Reitschulgasse 2), has a small but impressive collection of 19th–20th-century European art, including paintings by Cézanne, Courbet, Monet, Van Gogh and Edvard Munch. Among the sculptures are Rodin's *Gustav Mahler* and a Renoir *Venus.*

Most of the vast Habsburg fortune can be seen in the Hofburg. The **Schatzkammer** (treasury), in the Schweizerhof, contains a dazzling display of the insignia of the old Holy Roman Empire. These include the Imperial Crown of pure unalloyed gold set with pearls and unpolished emeralds, sapphires and rubies. First used in the year 962 for the coronation of Otto the Great in Rome, it moved on to Aachen and Frankfurt for crowning successors. Also on exhibit are the sword of Charlemagne and the Holy Lance, which dates back at least to the Merovingian kings and, supposedly,

pierced the body of Christ on the Cross.

If you visit the Schatzkammer in summer you may be able to catch a glimpse of a training session of the Spanish Riding School through the windows.

The **Hoftafel und Silberkammer** (Court China and Silver Collection), to the right of the Hofburg rotunda coming from the Michaelerplatz, exhibits the priceless Chinese, Japanese, French Sèvres and German Meissen services amassed by the Habsburgs in six centuries of wedding and birthday presents. Highlights are a 140-piece service in vermeil and a neo-Renaissance centrepiece given to Franz Joseph by Queen Victoria in 1851.

Perhaps the most Viennese collection in the Hofburg is the exquisite **Sammlung alter Musikinstrumente,** in the Neue Burg's National Library. There you'll find 360 pieces of great historical interest, particularly the Renaissance instruments which represent practically everything played up to the 17th century. Also on view: Haydn's harpsichord, Beethoven's piano of 1803 and an 1839 piano used by Schumann and Brahms.

In the end Vienna remains more a city of people than of objects and there are some fascinating museums devoted to its great men:

The **Schubert Museum** (Nussdorferstrasse 54), the house where the composer was

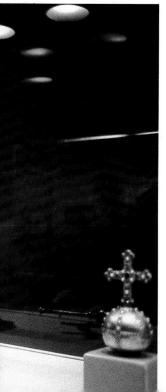

This magnificent bejewelled cross is part of the Habsburg treasury. **71**

born on January 31, 1797, has been lovingly restored.

The **Haydn Museum** is appropriately in Haydngasse (No. 19) where he composed his oratorios *The Creation* and *The Seasons*.

The **Beethoven Museum** is at Probusgasse 6 and the **Mozart Museum** is in the Figarohaus, Domgasse 5 (see p. 29).

The best arranged of these "personal" museums, making up for the hostility with which most Viennese received him during his lifetime, is the one devoted to **Sigmund Freud.** The house at Berggasse 19 has become a mecca for students—and patients—of psychoanalysis from all over the world. Freud lived here from 1891 until the arrival of the Nazis in 1938. A photograph in the museum shows the house subsequently draped with a swastika. All has been faithfully reconstituted by his disciples with original furniture and belongings, including his old hats, his walking stick and suitcases initialled S.F.

The **Vienna Tram Museum** *(Wiener Strassenbahnmuseum),* housed in the Erdberg depot (Erdbergstrasse 109), highlights the development of public transport, from horse-drawn tram to modern streetcar. (Open most weekends.)

Excursions

Danube Valley

One of the great attractions of Vienna is the fact that it embraces an enchanting countryside and is within easy reach of many other fascinating historic sites. If, however, your visit gives you time for only one side-trip it should unquestionably be along the Danube Valley, in particular the magical area known as the **Wachau,** preferably travelling north-east from Melk to Krems.

Just an hour's drive west of Vienna, this is the Austrian Danube's most picturesque landscape, by turns charming and smiling with its vineyards, apricot orchards and rustic villages, and then forbidding with ruined medieval castles and rocky cliffs half hidden in mists seemingly left there by centuries of Germanic saga. You cannot wax too romantic in describing the scenery, for this is the land of the Nibelungs, legendary inspiration for ruthless adventurers from the dawn of modern times, culminating in the heady exaltation and decadence of Wagnerian fantasy.

If you want to just sit and dream as this mythical world passes you by, take the Danube

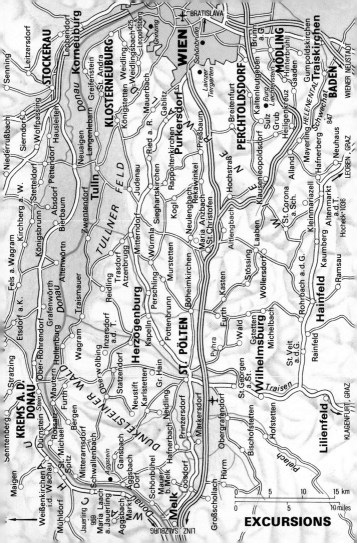

EXCURSIONS

river steamer (see p. 105), but for a closer look at the towns and castles on the way, do your touring by car.

One of the Nibelung stops may have been Medelike, today known as **Melk,** site of a superb Benedictine abbey towering over the River Danube. It is the perfect starting point (79 km. by the Westautobahn from Vienna) for a leisurely ride along the Danube Valley.

If the **abbey** *(Stift Melk)* looks uncommonly like a fortress it is because its strategic position high over a bend in the river made it a favoured point of defence from the time of the Romans. The Babenberg predecessors of the Habsburgs had a palace stronghold here in the 10th century which they handed over to the Benedictines in 1106. The monks gradually turned the sanctified fortress into a fortified sanctuary of noble proportions, gracefully enhanced by the baroque transformations of architect Jakob Prandtauer in 1702. Stretching along its trapezoid-shaped cliff top, the abbey softens the fierceness of its location with two elegant towers at its western end harmoniously grouped with the octagonal dome behind them and the lower Bibliothek and Marmorsaal to either side. The interior of the church is rich in reds and golds with a high altar by Antonio Beduzzi and superbly sculpted pulpit, choir and confessionals. The ceiling frescoes

Benedictine Abbey of Melk—a commanding presence on the Danube.

are by Johann Michael Rottmayr, whose work also adorns Vienna's Karlskirche.

Before crossing the Danube, it is worth making a quick trip to the village of MAUER (10 km. due east of Melk) to see the late-Gothic wooden altarpiece in the church, a truly miraculous marriage of craftsmanship and art. The work, by an anonymous local artist around 1500, depicts the adoration of the Virgin Mary with a wealth of detail and vivid figures.

You can now return, better armed, to the paganism of the crumbling castles on the Danube. Along the north bank, the Wachauer Strasse offers apri-

cot orchards and sunny vineyards, dotted with the 18th-century Weinhüterhütten (vine-guard's huts) to protect against grape-robbers, as well as villages featuring the early wine *(Heuriger)* in shaded courtyards. Then, on the opposite bank, you can see Schön-bühel and the ruins of Agg-stein, 12th-century homes of robber barons. Shiver a little.

In 1429 Aggstein was owned by Jörg Scheck vom Wald, popularly known as "Schreck-enwald" (Terror of the Forest). He led prisoners to his rose garden, on the edge of a sheer precipice, where they had the choice of starving to death or ending it quickly by jumping 175 feet to the rocks below. One night, one lucky knight escaped and told Duke Albrecht in Vienna about old Schrecken-wald. Albrecht promptly confiscated Aggstein—not to stop the mayhem but to cash in himself on the lucrative customs dues extorted from merchants.

Back on the happier north bank, visit the town of Spitz with its lovely late-Gothic **St. Mauritius church.** It's known for its apostle statues in the 1380 organ gallery and the baroque painting of the *Martyrdom of St. Mauritius* by Kremser Schmidt. In the village of St. Michael, look for seven stone hares perched on the roof of the 16th-century church. These commemorate a particularly vicious winter when snowdrifts were said to have enabled the animals to jump clear over the church. At Weissenkirchen is a fortified church (religion and war always went hand in hand in this region) which was surrounded by four towers, a moat, ramparts and 44 cannons to keep out the Turks.

The most romantic of these medieval towns is **Dürnstein,** famous as the site of Richard the Lion-Heart's imprisonment. Devastated by the Swedish army in 1645, the castle is more interesting to look at from below than to visit. But do see Dürnstein's bright and pleasant **abbey church,** a baroque structure with a splendid carved wooden door to the abbey courtyard and imposing statue of the resurrected Christ at the church entry.

Your journey along the Wachau will end delightfully with a visit to **Krems,** heart of the region's wine industry and historically one of the Danube Valley's most important trade

Minstrel Blondel saved his king with a timely song at Dürnstein.

A Song for Richard
During the Crusade of 1191, the brave but cheeky English king Richard the Lion-Heart enraged Leopold V von Babenberg by replacing the Austrian flag in Acre, Palestine, with the English one. Even worse, he prevented the Austrians from sharing in the booty. But, on his way home, though dressed as a peasant, Richard was recognized and thrown into the darkest dungeon of Dürnstein. He lingered there for several years until the faithful minstrel Blondel came looking for him, singing his favourite song. Richard revealed his place of imprisonment by joining in the chorus. His ransom—23,000 kilos of silver—was enough to finance the Holy Roman Empire's expedition to Sicily and to build a new wall around Vienna.

centres. Today, you can enjoy its superb Gothic, Renaissance and baroque residences on tranquil, tree-shaded squares —unspoiled by early 19th-century Biedermeier construction.

Park on the Südtiroler Platz and walk into this haven of peace through the old Steiner Tor with its Gothic pepperpot towers. Turn immediately left up the Schmidgasse to the Körnermarkt and the Dominikanerkirche (Dominican Church) transformed into an important museum of medieval art (look for the Grafenegg winged altarpiece). Continue round to the beautiful Pfarrplatz with its **church** redone (1616–30) by two Italian architects and graced by the masterful frescoes of Kremser (Martin Johann) Schmidt and altar paintings by Franz Anton Maulpertsch. The church epitomizes the town's own happy marriage of Italian and Austrian tastes.

Krems's oldest square, the Hoher Markt, boasts a masterpiece of Gothic residential architecture, the arcaded **Gozoburg,** built around 1270. Take a stroll on the Untere Landstrasse to see the elegant baroque façades (Nos. 41, 4 and 1) and the fine Renaissance **Rathaus** (town hall). Note its ornamented pentagonal bay window on the corner of Obere Landstrasse.

By now you will have earned a sip of the delicious light white wine in one of the leafy arcaded courtyards of the vaguely Tuscan inns along the Obere Landstrasse. The outstanding example of this 16th-century Italian Renaissance architecture is the Gasthof Alte Post (No. 32).

Let somebody else drive you (on route S3, 90 km.) back to Vienna.

Wienerwald

If the idea of Vienna is incomplete without the Danube, there would still be something missing if you left out the Wienerwald—and not just its northern slopes along the Höhenstrasse to Kahlenberg and Leopoldsberg. To properly appreciate the Wienerwald you must visit the villages hidden away in the forest to the south and southwest of Vienna. There, princes went hunting, composers wrote masterpieces and captains of industry could at last take a nap, away from the heat and bustle of the city.

Take the Breitenfurterstrasse (behind Schönbrunn Palace) out to PERCHTOLDSDORF, a serene little village amid heather-covered hills, vineyards and fir trees. Continue south to BURG LIECHTENSTEIN, recently built (1873) ruins of a castle on the site of the 12th-century home of the Liechtenstein dynasty. The park is a perfect place for a picnic. In **Mödling** you can see the 15th-century Gothic Spitalkirche and the house (Hauptstrasse 79) where Beethoven worked on his *Missa Solemnis.*

Turn west, along route 11, to HINTERBRÜHL, where the picturesque Höldrichsmühle, an old mill converted into an inn, is said to be the place where Schubert wrote his cycle of songs for the miller's daughter Rosi ("Die schöne Müllerin") in 1823. Actually the whole story originated in an 1864 operetta *Franz Schubert.*

The road takes you through gentle hills down to the Sattelbach Valley and the Cistercian Abbey of **Heiligenkreuz** (1135), the most important sanctuary founded by the Babenberg family. Heiligenkreuz (Holy Cross) is named after the relic of a piece of the True Cross, given to Austria by the King of Jerusalem in the 12th century, now kept in the tabernacle behind the high altar. You reach the basilica by a courtyard, which features a Trinity Column or Pestsäule (Pillar of the Plague) surrounded by plane trees. It's the work of baroque artist Giovanni Giuliani who also designed the basilica's splendid choir stalls. The structure has preserved the asymmetrical Romanesque western façade, and Giuliani's elegant work on the choir does not clash with the essential simplicity of the interior, a recognized triumph of spatial harmony in late-medieval architecture. You should also see, along the south side of the basilica, the graceful 13th-century cloister with 300 red columns.

In the town churchyard you'll find a tomb bearing the inscription: *"Wie eine Blume sprosst der Mensch auf und wird gebrochen"* ("Like a flower, the human being unfolds—and is broken.") It is the grave of Mary Vetsera, the 17-year-old girl who died in 1889 at Mayerling in a dual suicide with Crown Prince Rudolf, heir to the Austro-Hungarian Empire.

The scandalous event has been so enshrined in cheap romantic history and Hollywood hokum that it comes almost as a shock to see the actual signpost outside Heiligenkreuz pointing to MAYERLING, 3 kilometres to the west. The hunting lodge where the tragedy occurred was transformed, on the orders of Franz Joseph, into a Carmelite convent.

In the autumn of 1888, Rudolf, a bit of a libertine, fell in love with Mary, a daughter of the Hungarian Countess Vetsera. But the pope refused to annul the archduke's existing marriage. Angry with the conservative politics of his father Franz Joseph and miserable with his hopeless love affair, Rudolf decided, January 29, 1889, to spirit Mary away to his hunting lodge in Mayerling.

In the middle of the night Rudolf shot Mary with a revolver, covered her body with flowers and sat beside her till dawn, when he shot himself through the right temple—using a mirror so as not to miss.

To understand something of the world that was so shocked by the Mayerling drama, drive on through the beautiful Helenental Valley to the spa of

Baden. Enjoyed by the Romans and made fashionable by Franz I in 1803, Baden became the very symbol of upright Viennese Biedermeier prosperity. Occasionally taking the 36°C sulphurous waters to deal with a spot of rheumatism, the gentry of Vienna built their summer villas here and wandered in the spa's Kurpark to the strains of Johann Strauss's

Cistercian Abbey of Heiligenkreuz was founded in the 12th century with a piece of the True Cross brought from Jerusalem in the Crusades.

waltzes. The king of Biedermeier architecture was Josef Kornhäusel (see p. 34) and his neo-classical façades set the tone for the town's cozy conformity. The best example is his Ionic-porticoed Greek-temple Rathaus with Joseph Klieber's allegorical statues celebrating the ideals of the age: *Gerechtig-keit* (justice) and *Klugheit* (cleverness).

Once again time for a sip of wine. Drive home via **Gumpoldskirchen,** one of the prettiest of the wine villages with a lovely Gothic church, 16th-century town hall and cool, peaceful Heurigen wine-gardens.

To the East

The Bratislava road east from Vienna (Nr. 9) follows the Danube and traces the old Eastern European boundary of the Roman empire. Just 40 kilometres along you come to the remains of **Carnuntum,** capital of the Roman province of Pannonia, now attached to the town of PETRONELL. In the 2nd century, under Hadrian and Marcus Aurelius, it was a thriving commercial centre where Celtic amber merchants and gold-, silver- and coppersmiths lived in prosperous harmony with 6,000 Roman soldiers guarding the imperial outpost against barbarian invasion. Stop on the right before you reach the town

The bottle rarely stops moving—Gumpoldskirchen makes good wine.

and walk to the amphitheatre where spectators used to watch gladiators slaughter wild animals and each other. Today it's the site of a summer festival.

From Petronell drive south to **Rohrau,** the birthplace of Joseph Haydn. You can visit his beautifully restored thatched-roof house and perhaps be lucky enough to hear one of the concerts regularly

Pilgrims climb the steps of the Kalvarienberg church in Eisenstadt.

held there during spring and summer. Then stop by the Schloss Rohrau, residence of the Harrach family, early patrons of young Haydn. The castle has a fine collection of Spanish, Flemish and Italian art of the 17th century.

Continue on to one of Austria's most delightful lakes, the **Neusiedler See,** a birdwatchers' paradise teeming with heron, teal, waterfowl, wild geese, egret and many more. You could if you wished wade clear across the lake—only a few spots are more than 5 feet deep—but be sure to avoid the southern tip; that is in Hungary and strictly off limits. Flat-bottomed boats can be hired for fishing—pike, carp and perch —or duck-hunting. In winter there's skating and ice-sailing; in summer they perform operettas on the landing-stages. Austrians will put on operettas anywhere.

Along the lake's western shores are the villages of **Rust** and **Mörbisch.** Both are famous for the storks that favour their chimneys for nesting— Rust has nearly 50 stork-nests on its rooftops. In Mörbisch, right on the Hungarian border, don't miss the unspoiled shady lanes with spotless white-washed houses colourfully decorated with flowers and bouquets of maize. The wine gardens are positively idyllic.

On the way back to Vienna, you can pass through the baroque town of **Eisenstadt,** where Haydn lived and worked for many years in the service of Hungarian Prince Esterhazy. The composer is also buried there.

85

What to Do

Entertainment

There are people who wouldn't touch opera with a ten-foot pole—until they come to Vienna. Suddenly, in an atmosphere of sheer love, enthu-

siasm and excitement, that only the Viennese can muster, the most hardened resistance to this most challenging of musical forms just melts away. It's difficult to think of a cultural institution in another European capital that holds the privileged place of the **Staatsoper** (State Opera) in Vienna. Since this is Austria, try to make Mozart your first opera. A Vienna season without at least one in the repertory is unthinkable. Thereafter, you'll be ready to take on Wagner and even Alban Berg.

If you are lucky enough to have tickets for a première or other gala performance, you should wear evening dress, but even on an ordinary night you may want to wear a dinner jacket or long dress and you won't be the only ones. Opera in Vienna is always a celebration. Nobody will turn you away if you go in jeans, but it's almost as inappropriate as tennis shorts in the cathedral.

There's also first-rate opera to be heard at the **Volksoper** (Währingerstrasse 78), and operetta and ballet at the **Theater an der Wien** (Linke Wienzeile 6).

In the two principal concert halls—the **Musikverein** (Dumbastrasse 3), a sumptuously decorated masterpiece of acoustics, and the **Konzerthaus** (Lothringerstrasse 20)—you can hear the Vienna Philharmonic and Vienna Symphony Orchestras—still among the world's greatest, plus countless solo and chamber music recitals. You should also try to hear the celebrated Wiener Sängerknaben (Vienna Boys' Choir) who sing at Sunday Mass and other festivities in the Burgkapelle in the Hofburg.

Vienna has music for every taste but opera is the undisputed king.

Music in Vienna is not only that of its hallowed classical tradition, but also the joy of its

waltzes—music made famous around the world by Johann Strauss and his family. It can still be heard—and sometimes danced to—at afternoon and evening concerts in the Stadtpark and Prater-cafés and Wienerwald Heurigen. Or make for the *Johann Strauss* riverboat moored on the Danube Canal to listen and dance to Strauss and Lanner. The

more formal version can be enjoyed at the grand winter season balls—organized by associations of doctors, chemists, lawyers, engineers, even *Fiaker*—the highlight being the Kaiserball (Emperor's Ball, without the Emperor) on New Year's Eve in the Hofburg.

The major music season runs from September to June, climaxing with the **Vienna Festival** (end of May to end of June). In July and August, there are excellent summer

Miniature musicians play to an empty house at the Prater park.

concerts in the courtyard of the Rathaus and at Schönbrunn, Belvedere and other places around the city.

The **Burgtheater** is not just Vienna's proudest theatre but also one of the leading ensembles of the German-speaking world. The **Akademietheater** concentrates on modern and avant-garde drama.

For the Staatsoper, Volksoper, Burgtheater, Akademietheater and the Wiener Sängerknaben, you should reserve well in advance. See TICKETS in the Blueprint section.

Vienna also has its nightclubs, discothèques and cabarets, mostly around the Kärntnerstrasse, but the most typical light entertainment remains the sentimental violin and zither music of the Balkan restaurants, the Schrammelmusik of the Heurigen wine-gardens (see p. 98) or the oom-pah-pah brass of the Prater (see p. 56).

The Waltz

The waltz began as a heavy plodding triple-time German dance known as a *Ländler* which the Viennese transformed into a gay, whirling moment of fairyland. The man who brought the waltz to popular dance-halls in 1819 was Joseph Lanner, leader of a small band. After he added a young viola player named Johann Strauss, the waltz sprouted wings. The group grew to an orchestra and Strauss broke away to form his own—Lanner sadly celebrating the occasion with his "Trennungswalzer" (Separation Waltz).

The two conducted a prolonged "Waltz War" for public favour in the cafés of the Prater. The rivalry ended amicably and Strauss played waltzes—adagio—at Lanner's funeral.

89

Sports

With a foresight that nobody gives them credit for, the Habsburgs provided modern **joggers** with the perfect route, without even leaving the Innere Stadt. Start at the Burgtheater end of the Volksgarten near the monument to Empress Elisabeth, trot past the Theseus Temple, once around the duck pond to the statue of dramatist Franz Grillparzer and then across Heldenplatz past Archduke Karl and Prince Eugene. Skirt the edge of the Neue Hofburg and whip around the Burggarten to salute the monuments to Goethe and Mozart. Following all the paths, from Sissi to Wolfgang Amadeus and back, should take you less than 30 minutes.

There is indoor **swimming** at the Dianabad, near the Marienbrücke on the left bank of the Danube Canal. The best outdoor swimming is up north of Grinzing in the Krapfenwaldl (38S bus along Cobenzlgasse) or in the Alte Donau (the blue bit, remember) at the end of Moissigasse. You can also go **sailing** on the Alte Donau; details from the

There really is a blue Danube, the Alte Donau, ideal for watersports.

Austrian Yacht Club (Prinz-Eugen-Strasse 12).

Tennis players will find dozens of courts in the Prater at Rustenschacher Allee and in the Donaupark, Kratochwjlestrasse and Eiswerkstrasse. There is a huge **bowling** alley in the Prater (Hauptallee 124). The Freudenau area of the Prater has **horse-racing, polo** and plain **horse-riding.**

You can enjoy **ice-skating** year round in the Wiener Stadthalle in the 15th District (Vogelweidplatz 14).

There are some who prefer the Stadtpark for jogging—more musical, they say, taking a route round statues of Schubert, Bruckner and Johann Strauss across to Beethovenplatz...

Shopping

Not surprisingly the most important shopping attraction in Vienna—a town preoccupied by its history—is **antiques.** Furniture and objets d'art from all over the old empire have somehow ended up here in the little shops in the Innere Stadt around the Josefsplatz—Augustinerstrasse, Spiegelgasse, Plankengasse and Dorotheergasse. You can still find authentic rococo, Biedermeier and Jugendstil pieces, including **91** signed furniture of the great designers Michael Thonet and Josef Hoffmann.

Your best chance of finding a bargain is in the auction-rooms of the **Dorotheum** (Dorotheergasse 17). This state pawn-shop, popularly known as "Tante Dorothee" (Aunt Dorothy), was set up by Emperor Joseph I to enable the *"nouveaux pauvres"* to realize a quick return on heirlooms and possibly redeem them later in a more prosperous period. But it was also a kind of state-sponsored clearing-house for stolen art objects, where the original owners could even buy their property back, if the police had not managed to run down the thieves. The items are put on display before the sale, often in the windows of a bank opposite the auction rooms. If you feel uncertain about bidding, you can for a small fee hire a licensed agent to do it for you.

Still in the realm of the past are the great speciality shops for **coin-** and **stamp**-collectors (where else could you expect to find mint-condition Bosnia-Herzegovina issues of 1914?).

The national **Augarten porcelain** workshops still turn out hand-decorated rococo chinaware, including, of course, the Lipizzaner horses in action. **Petit-point embroidery** is available in the form of handbags, cushions and other items with flower, folk and opera motifs. Viennese craftsmen are also noted for their ceramics, handmade dolls, enamel miniatures and costume jewellery.

You will find the more elegant shops on the **Kärntnerstrasse, Graben** and **Kohlmarkt.** Austrian costume has caught the whimsical attention of high fashion with the Dirndl, the pleated skirt with blue or pink and white apron tied at the waist and white billowing-sleeved blouse under a laced bodice. For men the traditional heavy woollen Loden cloth makes excellent green or grey coats, cloaks and jackets. There are also good classic jackets and waistcoats in suede.

If your taste runs from the exquisite to High Kitsch, try your luck in the Saturday morning **flea market** on the Naschmarkt. It is situated next to the fruit and vegetable market at the Kettenbrückengasse underground station. Although the market tends to cater for youthful tastes, there's something for everyone here. Each week a different provincial town brings in its stuff and nonsense.

The Naschmarkt flea market is the international bazaar for everyone.

Wining and Dining

When it comes to Viennese cooking, you must bear in mind that this was the centre of the old Habsburg empire of 60 million Eastern and Southern Europeans and not just the capital of 7 million Austrians. The emperor and his archdukes and generals have gone but not the Bohemian dumplings, the Hungarian goulash, the Polish stuffed cabbage and Serbian shashlik, and the brandies of cherries and apricots and plums that accompany the Turkish coffee. The best wines, you'll be told, are local*.

Though there *are* Austrian specialities, the real adventures are in the culinary voyage you can make without budging outside the Ringstrasse—from Lombardy to Belgrade, to Budapest, to Prague, and to Warsaw.

But let's start with Austria anyway with two historic staples of the Viennese table that you're likely to come across immediately: the *Wienerschnitzel* —a large, very large, thinly

---

* For a comprehensive guide to wining and dining in Austria, consult the Berlitz EUROPEAN MENU READER.

sliced cutlet of veal crisply sautéed in a coating of egg and seasoned breadcrumbs—and *Wienerbackhendl*—boned roast chicken prepared in the same way. To be authentic, Viennese gourmets insist, the *Wiener-schnitzel* can be served only with cold potato salad or a cucumber salad. The *Backhendl* may be served with *Geröstete* sautéed potatoes.

The latter is an essential accompaniment, along with *Kren* (horseradish) and *Schnitt-lauchsauce* (chive sauce), to the most mystifying of Viennese delicacies, *Tafelspitz*. To foreigners this is nothing but boiled beef, to the natives it's apparently ambrosia. Order it only for lunch, they say, since by dinner time you may be getting what was prepared for midday, warmed over. Eat it fresh and you'll discover what kept Franz Joseph on the throne for 68 years—it was his favourite dish.

If your palate prefers something more spicy, you'll be glad Franz Joseph kept a hold on Hungary as long as he did. It made the goulash an inseparable part of the Vienna menu—beef chunks stewed in onions, garlic, paprika, with tomatoes and heart of celery, seasoned against that cold wind from the steppes. And the *Debrecziner*

sausage and the soups—*Köménymag Leves Nokedival* (caraway-seed soup with dumplings) or apple soup (apples, cloves, cinnamon, white wine, lemon-juice, sugar and thick, thick cream).

From Czechoslovakia comes delicious Prague ham and sauerkraut soup. From Polish Galicia, the roast goose served with dumplings and red cabbage. From Serbia, the peppery barbecued *cevapcici* meatballs and *schaschlik* brochettes of lamb with onion, green and red peppers.

Incidentally, many butcher shops have snackbars where you can get very good sausages, sandwiches, drinks and desserts.

Dumplings *(Knödel)*, a fixture of Austrian cooking, are served with soups and with the meat dish, studded with pieces of liver or bacon, or as a dessert with hot apricot inside *(Marillenknödel)* or with cream cheese *(Topfenknödel)*.

Hot desserts are a speciality. Try the *Palatschinken* from Hungary, pancakes filled with jam or nuts, or *Apfelstrudel*, thinly sliced apple with raisins and cinnamon rolled in an almost transparent, flaky pastry.

The word has slipped out. Pastry! Like Waltz, Woods, **96** Danube, inseparable from Vienna itself. The variations of cherries, strawberries, hazelnuts, walnuts, apple and chocolate in tarts, pies and cakes are endless. Have them *mit Schlag* (with whipped cream) or without, but have them. And join in the never-ending controversy over the most famous chocolate cake in the world, the Sacher-

torte—whether it should be split and where the apricot jam should go. They even fought a law case over who had the right to the label "original Sachertorte"—the venerable Hotel Sacher (on Philharmonikerstrasse) or the equally prestig-

At day's end, just take stock of it all in a cool quiet Kaffeehaus.

ious Konditorei Demel (Kohlmarkt 18). Sacher won. But
test the different versions yourself. They're almost all terrific,
mit or *ohne Schlag!*

Wines and Wine-Gardens

Wine in Vienna is almost always white wine, which the
Viennese drink quite happily
with meat and fish alike—the
only really decent reds being
the *Vöslauer,* from Bad Vöslau
near Baden, and the *Kalterer-
see,* imported from the South
Tyrol, now Italy's Alto Adige.
The best known of Austrian
white wines, the *Gumpolds-
kirchner,* has the good body
and bouquet of its southern
vineyards. But the Viennese
give equal favour to their own
*Grinzinger, Nussdorfer, Sieve-
ringer* and *Neustifter.* From the
Danube Valley, with an extra
natural sparkle, come the
Kremser, Dürnsteiner and *Lan-
genloiser.*

To enjoy them in their
original state, order these wines
herb (dry), as the producers often sweeten them for what they
imagine to be foreign tastes.

Perhaps the most pleasant
thing about Vienna's wines is
the way they are drunk. With
their talent for good living, the
Viennese have created a splendid institution—the *Heurigen*

—where you can sip white wine
on mild evenings under the
stars.

Wine-growers are allowed
by law to sell a certain amount
of their new wine—*Heuriger*—
directly to the public. They an-
nounce the new wine by hang-
ing out a pine branch. Then
people come to the tree-shaded
gardens and courtyards on the
slopes of the Wienerwald, sit-
ting at long scrubbed pinewood
tables, drinking and eating cold
meats and cheese, and listening
to the nostalgic Schrammelmusik of violins, guitars and
clarinette or accordion. When
the new wine has gone, the pine
branch must be withdrawn.

Heurigen of Grinzing are
very popular, but the best ones
remain the most peaceful—
and less easy to find—out in
Nussdorf, Ober-Sievering and
Neustift.

Beer is of course also a popular drink and the local *Gösser*
brew makes a worthy challenge
to the *Pilsner Urquell* imported
from Czechoslovakia. Among
the brandies you should try the
Hungarian *Barack* (apricot)
and Yugoslav *Slivovitz* (plum).

Coffee and the Kaffeehaus

And when all that wining and
dining is done, you may need a
good cup of coffee. In Vienna,

that's a whole way of life. First of all, you can't just go into a café and ask for a cup of coffee. The varieties are endless and there are names for all the shadings from black to white, each with its own personality. Ask for *einen kleinen Mokka* and you'll get a small strong black coffee and stamp yourself as someone of French or Italian taste. *Einen Kapuziner*, topped with whipped cream, is already more Viennese; *einen Braunen*, with just a dash of milk, entirely Viennese, sophisticated; *eine Melange* (pronounced "*me-lanksch*"), half milk, half coffee, designed for sensitive stomachs; *einen Einspänner* with whipped cream in a tall glass is for aunts on Sundays; *einen Türkischen*, prepared semi-sweet in a copper pot, for addicts of the Balkan Connection. In the 1920s the Café Herrenhof had a waiter who brought around a colour-chart with 20 variations of brown, and you ordered perhaps "*einen Dreizehner, mit Schlag*" (a 13 with cream) and he guaranteed satisfaction. Any coffee you order comes with a glass of water—just because Viennese water tastes so good.

The tradition of the Viennese *Kaffeehaus* dates back to the 17th century, when, so the story goes, a Hungarian opened Zum Roten Kreuz in the Domgasse with a stock of coffee beans captured from the Turks. By the time of Maria Theresa the town was full of coffee houses, fashionable and shady, where gentry and intellectuals mingled to pass the time of day in that leisurely *dolce-far-niente* so dear to the Viennese. Some developed their own particular clientele—painters, writers, politicians—while the most prominent (the Griensteidl, Café Central or the Herrenhof) brought them all together.

For many, the Kaffeehaus was a place to enjoy warmth and human contact rather than shiver in miserable lodgings. The need does not seem so pressing today, but a few *Kaffeehäuser* maintain the tradition: in the Innere Stadt, the Café Hawelka, popular with artists and antique dealers in the Dorotheergasse; Café Museum (Friedrichstrasse 6), where games of chess approach the ferocity of real war; and Café Sperl (Gumpendorfstrasse 11, in the 6th District), an elegant 100-year-old establishment with marble tables, Jugendstil chairs, an endless row of newspapers (including *The Times*, *Le Monde* and *La Stampa*) and billiard tables for those who cannot really bear to sit and do nothing.

To Help You Order...

Could we have a table?
Waiter!

Ich hätte gerne einen Tisch.
Herr Ober!

I would like...   **Ich möchte gerne...**

Beer	**ein Bier**	Menu	**die Karte**
Bread	**etwas Brot**	Milk	**Milch**
Butter	**etwas Butter**	Mineral	**Mineral-**
Cheese	**Käse**	water	**wasser**
Coffee	**einen Kaffee**	Mustard	**etwas Senf**
Dessert	**Nachspeise**	Potatoes	**Erdäpfel**
Eggs	**Eier**	Salad	**Salat**
Fish	**Fisch**	Salt	**Salz**
Fruit	**Obst**	Soup	**eine Suppe**
Glass	**ein Glas**	Sugar	**Zucker**
Ice-cream	**Gefrorenes**	Tea	**einen Tee**
Lemon	**Zitrone**	Vegetables	**Gemüse**
Meat	**Fleisch**	Wine	**Wein**

...and Read the Menu

Apfel	apple	**Knofel*/**	garlic
Beinfleisch	boiled beef	**Knoblauch**	
Birne	pear	**Kuchen**	cake
Ente	duck	**Lamm**	lamb
Erdbeeren	strawberries	**Nudeln**	noodles
Fisolen*/	green beans	**Obers*/**	cream
Bohnen		**Sahne**	
Forelle	trout	**Reis**	rice
Gekocht	boiled	**Rindfleisch**	beef
Geröstetes	sautéed potatoes	**Rostbraten**	roast beef
Geselchtes	smoked pork chops	**Salzburger**	omelet soufflé
		Nockerl	
mit Kraut	with sauer- kraut	**Schinken**	ham
Hendl	chicken	**Schwammerl*/**	mushrooms
Kalbfleisch	veal	**Pilze**	
Kalbshaxe	veal shank	**Schweine-**	pork
Kartoffel-	potato salad	**fleisch**	
salat		**Torte**	layer cake
Kirschen	cherries	**Wild**	game
		Wurst	sausage
		Zwiebeln	onions

* Austrian term

BLUEPRINT for a Perfect Trip

How to Get There

Although the fares and conditions described below have all been carefully checked, it is advisable to consult a travel agent for the latest information on fares and other arrangements.

BY AIR

Scheduled flights. There is regular service to Vienna from various centres in the U.K. Flying time from London is two and a half hours.

In addition to non-stop flights from New York, there is scheduled service from over 40 American cities as well as a dozen cities in Canada to European gateway destinations from which you can make connections to Vienna.

Charter flights. Cheap charter flights are available from the U.K. Generally, you find your own accommodation and pay the tour operator a nominal sum.

Charters are scheduled from a selection of North American cities, including ABC (Advance Booking Charter) flights good for two-, three- and four-week stays, and OTC (One-Stop Inclusive Tour Charter) package deals which include round-trip air transport, hotel accommodation, selected meals and sightseeing. In addition, dozens of American tour operators have individual and group packages to Austria offering stays of from two days to two weeks in Vienna. These tours are varied and feature food and wine, skiing, camping, art and architecture. Consult a reputable travel agent for all details of current programmes.

BY CAR

The quickest route to Vienna is via Ostend through Brussels, Cologne, Nuremburg and Linz, although there are more attractive routes through the countryside. The ferry crossings to Ostend leave from Dover and Folkestone.

You can also put your car on a train from Brussels to Salzburg, from which it's a three-hour drive on the *Autobahn* to Vienna.

BY RAIL

The Ostend-Vienna express takes about 16 hours; the whole trip, London to Vienna, would be about 24 hours. Couchettes and sleepers are available, but must be reserved in advance. The Inter-Rail Card is available to travellers under 26. The Rail Europ Senior Card is on sale in Europe and permits senior citizens to travel throughout Western Europe for one month. There's also the "Austria Ticket", which entitles the holder to unlimited travel for specific periods on train and postal buses, with reductions on certain boat trips on the Danube. Anyone under age 26 can obtain a "Junior Austria Ticket". These can be purchased at major rail stations in Austria or at travel agencies abroad.

Note: If you wish to travel around Europe extensively, buy a Eurailpass—a flat-rate, unlimited-mileage ticket good for first-class trains anywhere in Western Europe outside Great Britain. Eurail Youthpass is similar to the Eurailpass, but offers second-class travel at a cheaper rate to anyone under 26.

BY COACH

Europabus services connect London and Vienna in summer. However, overnight accommodation must be added to the cost of the trip.

When to Go

Spring is probably Vienna's most pleasant season. Chestnut trees and white lilac are in blossom and the city's music festival is in full swing. In July and August the town's residents take their summer holidays leaving the city freer for visitors, and then in September there's the opera and theatre season and the spectacular autumn colours of the Wienerwald. Even in winter Vienna can be worth the trip for a marvellous white Christmas, in spite of the cold east wind.

The following chart shows Vienna's average monthly temperatures:

	J	F	M	A	M	J	J	A	S	O	N	D
°F	30	33	40	50	58	64	68	67	61	51	41	34
°C	–1	1	5	10	15	18	20	19	16	10	5	1

Planning Your Budget

To give you an idea of what to expect, here is a list of average prices in Austrian schillings (S). They can only be approximate, however, as in Austria, too, inflation creeps relentlessly up.

Airport. Porter 15 S per bag. Bus to centre 55 S, Taxi 450–500 S.

Babysitters. 80–100 S per hour plus tram or taxi fare.

Bicycle and moped hire. Bicycle 200 S a day, moped 180–240 S per day plus 1 S per km.

Car hire. *VW Golf* 610 S a day plus 6.10 S per km. (1,500 S a day with unlimited mileage). *BMW 316* 800 S a day plus 8 S per km., 8,500 S per week with unlimited mileage. *Mercedes 300* 1,300 S a day plus 13 S per km., 15,000 S per week with unlimited mileage. Add 20% VAT and 1% contract fee.

Cigarettes. Austrian brands 20–40 S, foreign brands 35–55 S.

Entertainment. Cinema 60–110 S, nightclub 300–500 S, discotheque 120–200 S.

Guides. 1,200 S for half a day, 2,300 S per day.

Hairdressers. *Man's* haircut 110–210 S. *Woman's* haircut 130–220 S, shampoo and set 170–260 S, blow-dry 150–260 S, rinse/dye 150–370 S.

Hotels (double room with bath per night). ***** 2,200–4,000 S, **** 1,200–2,000 S, *** 800–1,200 S, ** 600–1,000 S, * (boarding house) 300–700 S.

Meals and drinks. Continental breakfast 65–100 S, lunch/dinner in fairly good establishment 250–500 S, coffee 20–50 S, beer 20–40 S, Austrian wine (bottle) 120–280 S, cocktail 70–110 S.

Public transport. 19 S for single ticket, 13 S for single ticket bought in advance (5 tickets minimum), 3-day ticket 92 S.

Sightseeing. Fiaker 350 S for a short sightseeing tour, 550 S for a long one. Danube River bus 160 S. Museums 15–45 S, Museum Pass 150 S.

Taxis. Meter starts at 22 S, plus 9.25 S per km.

Tickets. Concerts 70 (standing places) to 700 S, opera 70 S (standing room) to 1,800 S, Spanish Riding School 135 S (standing room) to 600 S, Burgkapelle (Vienna Boys' Choir) 60–180 S (standing room is free).

An A–Z Summary of Practical Information and Facts

> Listed after many entries is the appropriate German translation, usually in the singular, plus a number of phrases that should help you when seeking assistance. Additional phrases and expressions are to be found on p. 125.
> For prices, refer to list on p. 104.

AIRPORT *(Flughafen).* The Schwechat Airport, about 20 kilometres from the centre of Vienna, handles domestic and international flights. The modern building has a bank, restaurants, coffeebars, news and souvenir stands, a duty-free shop and the Vienna Airport Tourist Information Office (in the arrivals hall). This office can arrange your hotel accommodation and is open every day 24 hours a day.

A

   In addition to taxis, a bus circulates between the airport and Vienna. There are also rail connections. For details see PUBLIC TRANSPORT section.

BABYSITTERS *(Babysitter).* Although your hotel receptionist can sometimes arrange for a sitter, there are also agencies who have a list of multilingual babysitters. They are very reliable and some even have professional training:

B

Babysitter des Österreichischen Akademischen Gästedienstes, Mühlgasse 20, tel. 587-3525.

Babysitterzentrale, Herbststrasse 6–10, tel. 95 11 35.

Can you get me a babysitter for tonight?	**Können Sie mir für heute abend einen Babysitter besorgen?**

BOAT EXCURSIONS. Boats on the Danube River operate daily from the first of June to late September between Vienna and Krems, Krems and Melk, Melk and Linz, Linz and Passau. Steamers are equipped with a restaurant. Schedules and fares are available at most tourist offices or at the Austrian Danube Steamship Company. This company also organizes cruises from Vienna to Budapest, Belgrade and the Black Sea. For information and reservations contact:

Donau-Dampfschiffahrts-Gesellschaft,Handelskai 265, tel. 26 65 36. **105**

B   If you don't have time for one of the longer excursions, you can still get a feel of the river on a "Danube-bus" *(Donaubusse)* trip inside the city limits. Contact the Vienna Tourist Board for information. The boat leaves twice a day from Schwedenbrücke on a 3 hour trip.

C   **CAMPING**. Five major camping sites are located inside the city limits and one just outside. They are very well organized and offer every comfort. For details ask the Viennese Tourist Board for their brochure describing the campsites and their facilities. This brochure is also available from:

Österreichischer Camping Club (ÖCC), Johannesgasse 20, 1010 Vienna.

May we camp here?	**Dürfen wir hier zelten?**
Is there a campsite near here?	**Gibt es in der Nähe einen Campingplatz?**
We have a tent/caravan.	**Wir haben ein Zelt/einen Wohnwagen.**

CAR HIRE *(Autovermietung)*. You can arrange immediate hire upon arrival at Vienna's airport or railway station. Otherwise your hotel or the yellow pages of the telephone book have the addresses of leading firms. It's usually possible to have the car delivered to your hotel. Some firms permit the car to be returned to another European city.

To hire a car you'll need your driving license; minimum age is 21 years. Normally a deposit is charged when hiring a car, but holders of major credit cards are exempt. Special weekend and weekly unlimited mileage rates may be available. See sample prices on p. 103.

I'd like to rent a car (for today).	**Ich möchte (für heute) ein Auto mieten.**
for tomorrow	**für morgen**
for one day/for a week	**für einen Tag/für eine Woche**

CHILDREN'S ACTIVITIES. Following are some suggestions for outings with the kids—which parents, too, might appreciate for a change of pace:

Prater amusement park with bowling alleys, riding stables, roller coasters, merry-go-rounds and the biggest Ferris wheel in Europe.

Schönbrunn park with a zoo and coach collection (Wagenburg).

Boating on the Alte Donau where there are kayaks, rowing boats and sailing boats for rent.

Ice-skating on the indoor rink in the Stadthalle, Vogelweidplatz or, in season, on the outdoor rink at Lothringerstrasse 22 near the Inter-Continental Hotel.

Swimming in public indoor or outdoor pools in all parts of Vienna. Look for the list in the telephone book under "Badeanstalten".

CLOTHING *(Kleidung)*. Vienna's weather tends to be extreme—very hot in the summer and very cold in the winter—and the wind off the steppes can whip through at any time. Even in summer you should take a cardigan and a raincoat for the suddenly cooler evenings.

The Viennese like to dress up for the theatre, concert and opera, but a dark suit or cocktail dress is nearly always appropriate. Only in the most luxurious restaurants would a man be turned away without a tie and jacket. A dinner jacket (tuxedo) or evening dress is worn on special occasions, such as premières and galas. If you're shopping for clothes, refer to the chart below:

Men							
Clothing		**Shirts**		**Shoes**			
GB/USA	Aust.	GB/USA	Aust.	GB	USA	Aust.	
34	44	14	36	7	7½	40	
36	46	15	38	7½	8	41	
38	48	16	40	8	8½	42	
40	50	17	42	9	9½	43	
42	52	17½	43	10	10½	44	

Women								
Clothing			**Shirts/Pullovers**			**Shoes**		
GB	USA	Aust.	GB	USA	Aust.	GB	USA	Aust.
10	8	36	32	10	38			
12	10	38	34	12	40	4	5½	36
14	12	40	36	14	42	5	6½	37
16	14	42	38	16	44	6	7½	38
18	16	44	40	18	46	6½	8	38½
20	18	46	42	20	48	7	8½	39

C **COMPLAINTS** *(Reklamationen)*. Despite a historically lackadaisical reputation, modern Vienna is remarkably efficient. But if something should go wrong and neither you nor the famous Viennese charm can help to put it right, you should report the matter to the Vienna Tourist Board. See TOURIST INFORMATION.

In hotels, restaurants and shops, complaints can be made to the manager or proprietor; try to stay calm and courteous. For more serious affairs do not hesitate to contact the police or your consulate.

CONVERTER CHARTS. For fluid, tire pressure and distance measures, see page 111. Austria uses the metric system.

Temperature

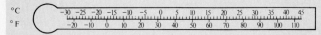

Length

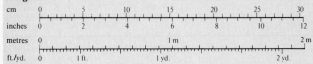

Weight

COURTESIES. Among themselves the Viennese have developed an elaborate system of courtesy—a left-over from the Habsburg days—in which they call each other by academic, bureaucratic and aristocratic titles, sometimes even when unwarranted. You will probably not get involved in this, but do not be surprised—if you are a woman—to hear yourself regularly addressed as *Gnädige Frau* (gracious lady) with the additional *Küss die Hand* (I kiss your hand); sometimes the hand is actually kissed! Introductions to people are always accompanied by a handshake.

When you go into a shop it is customary to say *guten Tag* (good day) or *guten Abend* (good evening) before making your request and, of course, *auf Wiedersehen* (good-bye) when you leave. To a close friend you can say *Servus* instead of *auf Wiedersehen*. See also MEETING PEOPLE.

CRIME and THEFT. Compared to most parts of the world, Austria's crime and theft rate is quite low. Nonetheless it is advisable not to leave valuable objects in view in your car, which should in any case be locked.

If you have been robbed, do not hesitate to go to the nearest police station (see POLICE). If your passport is stolen, the police will give you a certificate to take to your consulate.

I want to report a theft.	**Ich möchte einen Diebstahl melden.**
My handbag/wallet has been stolen.	**Meine Handtasche/meine Brieftasche ist gestohlen worden.**

CUSTOMS FORMALITIES *(Zoll).* Following are the items you can take into Austria duty free (if you are over 17 years of age) and then back into your own country.

Into:	Cigarettes	Cigars	Tobacco	Spirits	Wine
Austria 1)	200 or	50 or	250 g.	1 l. and	2 l.
2)	400 or	100 or	500 g.	1 l. and	2 l.
Australia	200 or	250 g. or	250 g.	1 l. or	1 l.
Canada	200 and	50 and	900 g.	1.1 l. or	1.1 l.
Eire	200 or	50 or	250 g.	1 l. and	2 l.
N. Zealand	200 or	50 or	250 g.	1.1 l. and	4.5 l.
S. Africa	400 and	50 and	250 g.	1 l. and	2 l.
U.K.	200 or	50 or	250 g.	1 l. and	2 l.
U.S.A.	200 and	100 and	3)	1 l. or	1 l.

1) Arriving from European countries.
2) Arriving from non-European countries.
3) A reasonable quantity.

Tourists do not pay duty on personal jewellery, sports equipment (for personal use), gifts and souvenirs up to a value of 400 schillings.

Currency restrictions: Foreign and Austrian money can be taken into Austria without restriction. You can export 50,000 schillings in Austrian currency and an unlimited amount of foreign currency.

C **VAT reimbursement:** For purchases of more than 1,000 schillings you can have the value-added tax (sales tax) or *Mehrwertsteuer* reimbursed if you are taking the goods out of the country. The salesperson fills out a form (called "U 34") with your home address, passport number and the price. At the border a customs official will stamp this form which you must then mail to the shop for reimbursement by cheque or bank-order. You can also get a reimbursement at the border if you are travelling by car: stop at the Austrian Automobile Club office (ÖAMTC) and present the stamped form.

I've nothing to declare.	**Ich habe nichts zu verzollen.**
It's for my personal use.	**Das ist für meinen persönlichen Gebrauch.**

D **DRIVING IN AUSTRIA.** To bring your car into Austria you will need:

- International driving licence (your national licence for Europeans)
- Car registration papers
- National identity sticker for your car
- Red warning triangle in case of breakdown
- First-aid kit

For visitors who want to hire a car in Austria, see CAR HIRE section.

Driving regulations: Drive on the right, pass on the left. Although drivers in Austria follow the same basic rules which apply in other countries that drive on the right, some rules might be different.

- you must wear seat-belts;
- children under the age of 12 may not sit in front;
- on the motorway *(Autobahn)* passing another vehicle on the right is prohibited;
- vehicles coming from the right have priority at crossroads without other signals;
- trams have priority, even when coming from the left;
- vehicles must halt behind trams when they are slowing down to stop, loading or unloading passengers;
- it is prohibited to use your horn (day or night) in town.
- motorcyclists must wear crash helmets and use dipped headlights throughout the day.

Drunken driving is a very serious offence in Austria. The permissible alcohol level in the blood is 0.8 per mille.

Speed limits: On motorways (expressways) 130 kph (81 mph) or 100 kph (62 mph); on other roads 100 kph or 80 kph (50 mph); in built-up areas 50 kph (31 mph); with caravan (trailer) 80 kph on the open road; with studded tires 100 kph on motorways, 80 kph on other roads.

Parking: In streets with tram tracks, parking is prohibited from 8 p.m. to 5 a.m. from mid-December to end March. In fact, if at all possible, you should use public transport within the Gürtel (outer ring road) since one-way streets and traffic jams add confusion within the city where there's a real lack of parking space. To park in "blue" zones you'll need parking tickets, in use from 8 a.m. to 6 p.m. for up to 90 minutes. Tickets are available in banks and tobacco shops *(Tabak-Trafik)*.

Breakdowns: Austrian automobile clubs offer 24-hour breakdown service to all drivers on motorways and main roads: for the ÖAMTC call 120 or 95 40; for the ARBÖ call 65 58 65.

Fuel and oil: There are plenty of stations, some of them self-service. In Vienna, most service stations close at night, but you can get fuel very late at highway entrances to the city.

Distance

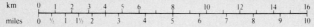

Fluid measures

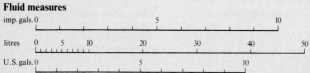

Tire Pressure

lb./sq.in.	kg/cm²	lb./sq.in.	kg/cm²
10	0.7	26	1.8
12	0.8	27	1.9
15	1.1	28	2.0
18	1.3	30	2.1
20	1.4	33	2.3
21	1.5	36	2.5
23	1.6	38	2.7
24	1.7	40	2.8

D **Road signs:** Most road signs employed in Austria are international pictographs but here are some written signs you might come across:

Anfang	(Parking) Start	**Ortsende**	Town ends
Ausfahrt	Exit	**Parken erlaubt**	Parking allowed
Aussicht	Viewpoint	**Rechts, links**	Turn right, left
Bauarbeiten	Road works	**einbiegen**	
Einbahn	One way	**Rollsplitt**	Loose gravel
Ende	(Parking) End	**Sackgasse**	Dead end street
Fahrbahnwechsel	Change lanes	**Spital**	Hospital
Fußgänger	Pedestrians	**Steinschlag**	Falling stones
Gefährlich	Danger	**Umleitung**	Diversion
Geradeaus	Straight on		(detour)
Glatteis	Slippery roads	**Vorfahrt**	Priority
Halten ver-	No stopping	**Vorsicht**	Caution
boten		**Werktags von**	Weekdays 7 a.m.
Licht ein-	Use headlights	**7 bis 17 Uhr**	to 5 p.m.
schalten		**Zufahrt gestattet**	Entry permitted

driving licence	**Führerschein**
car registration papers	**Zulassungsschein**
green card	**Grüne Karte**
Where's the nearest car park?	**Wo ist der nächste Parkplatz?**
Can I park here?	**Kann ich hier parken?**
Are we on the right road for…?	**Sind wir auf der richtigen Strasse nach…?**
Fill it up, please.	**Bitte volltanken.**
Check the oil/tires/battery, please.	**Öl/Reifen/Batterie prüfen, bitte.**
I've had a breakdown.	**Ich habe eine Panne.**
There's been an accident.	**Es ist ein Unfall passiert.**

E **EMBASSIES and CONSULATES** *(Botschaft; Konsulat).* Following is a list of embassies and consulates in Vienna:

Australia: Mattiellistrasse 2–4, 1040 Vienna, tel. 512 85 80.

Canada: Dr. Karl-Lueger-Ring 10, 1010 Vienna, tel. 533-36 91.

Eire: Landstrasser Hauptstrasse 2, 1030 Vienna, tel. 75 42 46.

New Zealand: Lugeck 1, 1010 Vienna, tel. 52 66 36.

South Africa: Sandgasse 33, 1190 Vienna, tel. (embassy) 32 64 930 (consulate) 75 61 17.

United Kingdom: Reisnerstrasse 40, 1030 Vienna, tel. 75 61 17.

U.S.A.: (embassy) Boltzmanngasse 16, 1090 Vienna, tel. 31 55 11; (consulate) Gartenbaupromenade 2, 1010 Vienna, tel. 51 451.

EMERGENCIES *(Notfälle).* If your hotel receptionist isn't at hand, the Viennese telephone service has several emergency numbers; the most important ones are listed below. If you speak no German, try in English or find someone who speaks English to help you call. See also MEDICAL CARE.

Police emergency	133
Assistance on the road	120, 123
Fire	122
Ambulance, first aid	144
Chemist (pharmacist) on duty	15 50
Emergency medical service	141

I need a doctor/dentist.	**Ich brauche einen Arzt/Zahnarzt.**
ambulance	**Krankenwagen**
fever	**Fieber**
toothache	**Zahnschmerzen**
Fire!	**Feuer!**
Help!	**Hilfe!**
hospital	**Spital**
police	**Polizei**

GUIDES and INTERPRETERS *(Fremdenführer; Dolmetscher).* The most romantic tour of Vienna is the famous horse-drawn cab. These *Fiaker* are usually parked at the Heldenplatz, Stephansplatz or near the Albertina and will take you around the major sightseeing spots. Make sure you agree on the cost of the trip before you begin (see p. 104) since this can vary depending on the time of day and the chosen itinerary.

Most hotels can arrange for multilingual guides or interpreters for any occasion. Or you can contact:

Travel Point, Boltzmanngasse 19, 1090 Vienna, tel. 31 42 43.

We'd like an English-speaking guide.	**Wir möchten einen englisch-sprachigen Fremdenführer.**
I need an English interpreter.	**Ich brauche einen Dolmetscher für Englisch.**
How long will the ride take?	**Wie lange dauert die Fahrt?**
What does it cost?	**Was kostet es?**

H **HAIRDRESSERS'** *(Friseur)*. It's wise to telephone for an appointment at women's hairdressers' *(Damenfriseur)* although there are many in Vienna. Prices range from *haute-coiffure* rates in the city centre to very reasonable beyond the Ring.

Most hairdressers' and barbers' *(Herrenfriseur)* are closed on Saturday afternoons and Mondays, with a few exceptions in the centre of town and at the railway station.

Not too much off (here).	**(Hier) nicht zu kurz schneiden.**
A little more off (here).	**(Hier) ein wenig kürzer schneiden.**
a colour chart	**eine Farbtafel**
a colour rinse	**eine Farbspülung**
a blow-dry (brushing)	**Föntrocknen**
a shampoo and set	**Waschen und Legen**
a haircut	**ein Haarschnitt**
a shave	**Rasieren**

HOTELS and ACCOMMODATION. The Vienna tourist office publishes an annual list of hotels, boarding houses and "seasonal" hotels (student hostels used as hotels from July to September) with details about amenities, prices and classifications. You can get it from the Austrian tourist office in your country or from travel agents. The tourist information bureaus (Opernpassage, on the south and west motorway entrances to Vienna, at the airport and the stations) can make room arrangements for you.

The personal atmosphere of boarding houses in Vienna makes them popular for longer stays. During spring, summer, early autumn and longer holidays such as Christmas and Easter, it is always advisable to book ahead. The famous old luxury hotels around the opera are often filled up and sometimes don't accept credit cards (most other hotels do). If you do not make use of your reservation, the hotel has a right to a cancellation fee.

Prices indicated on page 104 include service and, most often, breakfast.

a boarding house	**eine Pension**
a single/double room	**ein Einzel-/Doppelzimmer**
with/without bath (shower)	**mit/ohne Bad (Dusche)**
What's the rate per night?	**Was kostet eine Übernachtung?**

HOURS. Most small shops are open from 9 a.m. (food shops an hour earlier) to 6 p.m. with a break for lunch. Major department stores do business from 8 a.m. to 6 p.m. non-stop, but supermarkets close for about two hours at lunch. Saturday afternoons shops are closed.

Museum hours vary considerably, but the majority open from 9 or 10 a.m. to 3 or 4 p.m. weekdays, 9 a.m. to 1 p.m. on Saturdays and Sundays and close on Mondays.

Banks do business Mondays to Fridays from 8 a.m. to 3 p.m. (Thursdays until 5.30 p.m.). Branches usually close between 12.30 and 1.30 p.m.

Post offices are open Mondays to Fridays, 8 a.m. to 6 p.m. For post offices which offer 24-hour service see section POST OFFICE.

Chemists' are open from 8 a.m. to noon and from 2 p.m. to 6 p.m.; Saturday from 8 a.m. to noon.

LANGUAGE. Austria is, of course, German-speaking, but English is also very widely understood and spoken. If you don't speak German, don't forget to ask *"Sprechen Sie englisch?"* before plunging ahead.

The Berlitz phrase book, GERMAN FOR TRAVELLERS, covers most situations you're likely to encounter in Austria.

See also COURTESIES.

Do you speak English? **Sprechen Sie Englisch?**

LAUNDRY and DRY CLEANING. The advantage of getting your laundry washed or cleaned by the hotel is quick service, but the prices are high. Therefore it is worth seeking out neighbourhood dry-cleaners and self-service laundries. There are some laundries which do your clothes the same day. The yellow pages list addresses under "Wäschereien" (laundries) and "Putzereien" (dry cleaners), or your hotel receptionist will help you to find the nearest establishment.

When will it be ready? **Wann ist es fertig?**
For tomorrow morning, please. **Bis morgen früh, bitte.**

LOST PROPERTY *(Fundamt)*. If you have mislaid or lost something you should call or go to the lost property office:

Wasagasse 22, tel. 31 66 11-0.

Articles lost in trams or buses are turned in at the lost property office after 3 days (prior to that, call Vienna Transport at 65 9 30-0). If you **115**

L have forgotten something in a taxi, try the *Funk-Taxi* (radio taxi) numbers. For objects lost in the train, contact the central collecting office for the Austrian Railways:

Zentralsammelstelle der Österreichischen Bundesbahnen, Langauergasse 2, Westbahnhof, tel. 5650-2996.

I've lost my passport/wallet/handbag.	**Ich habe meinen Pass/meine Brieftasche/meine Handtasche verloren.**

M **MEDICAL CARE** *(Ärztliche Hilfe).* See also EMERGENCIES. Ask your insurance company before leaving home if medical treatment in Austria is covered by your policy.

Most chemists' or drugstores *(Apotheke)* are open Monday to Friday and Saturday morning (see HOURS). For night and Sunday service, all chemists' display the address of the nearest shop remaining on duty. Telephone number 15 50 to find out which chemist shops are open.

Where is there a chemist shop on duty?	**Wo ist die diensthabende Apotheke?**

MEETING PEOPLE. See also COURTESIES. The city's traditionally fashionable promenade streets—Kärntnerstrasse and the Graben—have been transformed into pedestrian zones. At all times of the year, but especially at weekends, those two streets are lively and bustling and in summer their open-air cafés are ideal meeting places. A good spot to get to know and talk with Viennese people is at the Heurigen taverns (see WINING AND DINING p. 98). There, without any formality you can join total strangers at the long tables for a glass of wine.

MONEY *(Geld).* See also PLANNING YOUR BUDGET, page 104. Austria's monetary unit is the *Schilling,* abbreviated *S, ÖS* or *Sch.,* divided into *Groschen* (abbreviated *g.*). Coins come in pieces of 1, 5, 10, 20, 25, 50, 100 and 1,000 schillings (the last in gold; essentially a collector's item) and 10 and 50 groschen. Be sure you don't confuse the similar 5- and 10-schilling pieces. There are banknotes of 20, 50, 100, 500 and 1000 schillings.

Banks and Currency Exchange *(Bank; Wechselstube)*. Foreign currency
can be changed in practically all banks and savings banks *(Sparkasse)*.
You can also change money at travel agencies and hotels, but the rate
will not be as good. See also HOURS section.

Some exchange offices are open on weekends at the airport, Südbahnhof, Westbahnhof, Air Terminal, Stephansplatz and Opernpassage. They're open from early morning (some from 6.30) until late
afternoon or evening every day of the week. Note that all post offices
cash eurocheques.

Traveller's cheques *(Reisescheck)* are welcome almost everywhere; but,
again, the rates are best in banks or exchange offices.

I want to change some pounds/dollars.	**Ich möchte Pfund/Dollar wechseln.**
Do you accept traveller's cheques?	**Nehmen Sie Reiseschecks an?**
Do you have any change, please?	**Haben Sie Kleingeld, bitte?**

PHOTOGRAPHY. Many museums allow you to take photographs
(sometimes for a small fee) but never with tripod or flash.

All popular film makes and sizes are available in Austria, but
developing colour film may take a week or more.

I'd like a film for this camera.	**Ich möchte einen Film für diese Kamera.**
a black and white film	**ein Schwarzweissfilm**
a film for colour prints	**ein Farbfilm**
a colour-slide film	**ein Diafilm**
a 35-mm film	**ein Fünfunddreissig-Millimeter-Film**
a super-8 film	**ein Super-Acht-Film**
How long will it take for this film to be developed?	**Wie lange dauert es, diesen Film zu entwickeln?**
Can I take a picture?	**Darf ich ein Foto machen?**

POLICE *(Polizei)*. Vienna's police wear green caps and jackets with
black trousers and drive white cars. Traffic police wear white caps
and, in summer, white jackets. Street parking is supervised by *"Poli-
tessen"* (meter-maids) in blue jackets and white hats. Police on

P motorcycles are popularly known as "white mice" *(weisse Mäuse)*. If you are fined for any reason, the police have the right to ask you to pay on the spot.

You can find the number for the various district police stations *(Bezirkspolizeikommissariat)* in the telephone book but in emergencies call 133.

Where is the nearest police station?	**Wo ist die nächste Polizei-Wachstube?**

POST OFFICE *(Postamt)*. Apart from the regular post office hours in most branches, the post offices at the main railway stations (Westbahnhof, Südbahnhof and Franz Josefs-Bahnhof) are open day and night, including Sundays and public holidays. Other post offices offering a 7-day-a-week, 24-hour service for registered, air and express mail (with a small extra charge for after-hours service) are:
Central Post Office, Fleischmarkt 19 and Central Telegraph Office, Börseplatz 1. For information call 832101.

Stamps and information about postage rates are also available at tobacco shops.

Mail: If you want to receive mail by poste restante (general delivery), have it sent as follows:

> Ms. Jane Smith
> Hauptpostlagernd
> Fleischmarkt 19
> 1010 Vienna, Austria

Do not forget your passport as identification when you go to pick up your mail.

Telegrams: The minimum for a regular telegram is 7 words. Nightletters *(Brieftelegramm)* are transmitted as a telegram delivered to the address with the normal mail of the day. One word costs half the price of the regular telegram rate (minimum 22 words).

express (special delivery)	**Express**
airmail	**Luftpost**
Have you any mail for…?	**Haben Sie Post für…?**
A stamp for this letter/post card, please.	**Eine Marke für diesen Brief/diese Postkarte, bitte.**
I want to send a telegram to…	**Ich möchte ein Telegramm nach… schicken.**

PUBLIC HOLIDAYS *(Feiertage)*. Austria observes 14 public holidays a year on which banks, museums, official services and many restaurants are closed. On Good Friday, a holiday for Protestants only, shops remain open.

January 1	*Neujahrstag*	New Year's Day
January 6	*Heilige Drei Könige*	Twelfth Night
May 1	*Staatsfeiertag*	Labour Day
	(Tag der Arbeit)	
August 15	*Mariä Himmelfahrt*	Assumption
October 26	*Nationalfeiertag*	National Holiday
	(Tag der Fahne)	(Flag Day)
November 1	*Allerheiligen*	All Saints' Day
December 8	*Unbefleckte*	Immaculate
	Empfängnis	Conception
December 25	*Weihnachten*	Christmas Day
December 26	*Stefanstag*	St. Stephen's Day
Movable dates:	*Karfreitag*	Good Friday
	Ostermontag	Easter Monday
	Christi Himmelfahrt	Ascension Day
	Pfingstmontag	Whit Monday
	Fronleichnam	Corpus Christi

On December 24, Christmas Eve, theatres and cinemas are closed all day and shops, restaurants and coffee houses close at midday.

Are you open tomorrow? **Haben Sie morgen geöffnet?**

PUBLIC TRANSPORT. Maps for buses, trams and the underground are available at main stops as well as at the central public transport information office at Karlsplatz.

Tickets can be bought from a conductor or a machine on trams and buses, from the booking office or machine for the main-line or city trains. There are different types of tickets available; the flat rate, the same for tram, train, underground (subway) travel and all bus services, is good for changes made without interruption. Books of five tickets (at a discount) can be bought in advance from a tobacconist's *(Tabak-Trafik)* or the transport offices *(Verkehrsbetriebe)*. Three- and 8-day tickets with which you can travel anywhere in Vienna are also available.

P **Trams** *(Strassenbahn):* Vienna has about 35 tram routes, making this the most important form of public transport. Trams are usually red and white. On most trams (and buses) the driver serves as conductor. These vehicles carry a blue sign at the front and rear with the word *Schaffnerlos* ("without conductor"). If you already have a ticket, enter the tram by the door marked *Entwerter* and have it stamped, otherwise get in at the front and buy your ticket from the vending machine. For trams with conductors, enter at the rear to buy a ticket or have it stamped.

Buses: Flat-rate tickets are valid on buses marked "A" or "B" but not actually issued on "B" buses. All other types of passes are also valid on buses in Vienna.

The airport bus service runs between the city air terminal at Landstrasser Hauptstrasse (the Hilton Hotel) and the airport every 20 or 30 minutes. The ride between the airport and the city takes about half an hour.

U-Bahn (underground/subway): Three lines operate at present, providing service to the main points in town. Tickets can be purchased from machines or ticket offices.

Stadtbahn (metropolitan): The trans-city rail service runs partly underground.

Schnellbahn (rapid-transit): Suburban trains depart from the Südbahnhof for certain outlying districts. The unit fare applies in the central zone, standard fares outside.

R **RELIGIOUS SERVICES.** Austria is predominantly Roman Catholic, but a good number of other denominations and faiths hold services regularly. Sunday mass in most churches is accompanied by orchestral and choral works.

T **TAXIS** *(Taxi).* Vienna's taxis can be caught directly at a rank, at busy locations throughout Vienna (such as at the main railway stations), or you can hail one in the street. There are never enough taxis at rush hour, so it would be wise to book in advance through your hotel receptionist or by phoning one of the following numbers:

31 30; 43 69; 60 160; or 91 01.

If you want to go beyond the city limits the fare should be discussed beforehand. See rates on page 104.

TELEPHONE *(Fernsprecher).* Glass-enclosed booths are scattered throughout the city. They can be recognized by a sign with a black receiver in a yellow circle on the door, and the word *Fernsprecher.*

The booths all have multilingual instructions. Some phone boxes are equipped for long-distance calls (considerably cheaper for calls inside Austria at night, on Saturday afternoons and Sundays). Note that on certain old-style telephones, a red button has to be pressed for connection the moment your party answers.

Note that surcharges on long-distance calls made from hotels are high. To keep costs down, go to the nearest post office or use any suitable public payphone, even for overseas.

Information operator for Austria:	16
Operator for foreign area codes and direct dialling:	08
Operator for abroad:	09

You'll find all the other important numbers on the first page of the telephone book. The front pages show you the area codes and telephone-rates.

TICKETS *(Karten).* Apart from the following specific addresses, tickets for different performances can be obtained at private ticket agencies *(Theaterkartenbüro)* all over the city as well as at major hotels. These will cost about 10 to 30 per cent more.

Concerts. Tickets are usually sold by subscription, and are rarely available at the box office or by post. To book the occasional seat available to the public contact:

Wiener Philharmoniker, Bösendorferstrasse 12, 1010 Vienna (often sold out) and Musikalische Jugend, same address as above.

Spanish Riding School. Tickets for the Sunday performances can be bought (preferably well in advance) from:

Spanische Reitschule, Hofburg, Michaelerplatz 1, 1010 Vienna.

Opera and Theatre. The best place for opera tickets is the national theatre ticket office *(Österreichischer Bundestheaterverband, Bestellbüro).* They sell tickets seven days ahead for opera *(Staatsoper),* operetta *(Volksoper),* Burgtheater and Akademietheater performances (closed in July and August); from outside Vienna you can reserve tickets to these four theatres at least 14 days before the performance by contacting the same address:

Bundestheaterkassen, Hanuschgasse 3/Goethegasse 1, 1010 Vienna, tel. 51 444. The box office is open from 9 a.m. to 5 p.m.

T **Vienna Boys' Choir** *(Wiener Sängerknaben)*. Obtain tickets in advance at the Hofburg Kapelle on Fridays from 5 to 7 p.m. for Sunday performances, or reserve several weeks in advance from:

Verwaltung der Hofmusikkapelle, Hofburg, Schweizerhof, 1010 Vienna.

TIME DIFFERENCES. Austria follows Central European Time (GMT + 1). In summer, clocks move ahead one hour, and the time difference looks like this:

New York	London	**Vienna**	Jo'burg	Sydney	Auckland
6 a.m.	11 a.m.	**noon**	noon	8 p.m.	10 p.m.

TIPPING. Since a service charge is included in hotel and restaurant bills, tipping is not obligatory. However, it's appropriate to give something extra to porters, cloakroom attendants, etc., for their services. The chart below makes some suggestions as to how much to leave.

Hotel porter, per bag	5–10 S
Maid, per week	50 S
Waiter	5% (optional)
Lavatory attendant	5 S
Taxi driver	10%
Tour guide	10%
Barber / Hairdresser	10–15%
Theatre usher	5 S

TOILETS *(Toiletten)*. Public facilities can be found near important streets or squares, often in the pedestrian underpasses. Normally toilets in cafés can be used without ordering anything but it's always more courteous to have a coffee or a beer.

If hand towels and soap are used, there is often a set fee rather than just a tip. Have a couple of schillings ready in case the door has a "slot" machine.

Toilets may be labelled with symbols of a man and a woman, the initials W.C., or with *Damen* (Ladies) and *Herren* (Gentlemen).

Where are the toilets? **Wo sind die Toiletten?**

TOURIST INFORMATION. See also AIRPORT. The Austrian National Tourist Office *(Österreichische Fremdenverkehrswerbung)*, a non-commercial organization (which cannot make reservations), has representatives in many countries (see list below). They can inform you about what to see, when to go and where to stay in and around Vienna:

Australia: A.N.T.O., 19th Floor, 1 York Street, Sydney 2000, NSW, tel. 27 85 81.

Canada: A.N.T.O., 2 Bloor Street East, Suite 3330, Toronto, Ont. M4W 1A8, tel. (416) 967-3381.

Eire: A.N.T.O., The Lodge, Ardoyne House, Pembroke Park, Ballsbridge, Dublin 4, tel. 68 33 21.

Great Britain: A.N.T.O., 30 St. George Street, London W1R 0AL, tel. (01) 62 90 461.

South Africa: A.N.T.O., 11 Eton Road, Parktown, Johannesburg.

U.S.A.: A.N.T.O., 500 Fifth Avenue, Suite 2009–2022, New York, NY 10110, tel. (212) 944-6880.

A.N.T.O., 11601 Wilshire Blvd., Suite 2480, Los Angeles, CA 90025, tel. (213) 477-3332.

A.N.T.O., 4800 San Felipe Street, Suite 500, Houston, TX 77056, tel. (713) 850-9999.

Or get in touch with one of the following:

Vienna Tourist Board *(Wiener Fremdenverkehrsverband)*, Kinderspitalgasse 5, 1095 Vienna, tel. 42 42 25 (phone service seven days a week).

Bureaus are also located in the Opernpassage (pedestrian subway near the Opera), in the Westbahnhof and Südbahnhof and at the airport.

Austria Information Centre *(Österreich-Information)*: Margaretenstrasse 1, 1040 Vienna, tel. 587 2000.

TRAINS *(Zug)*. The main railway stations in Vienna are the Westbahnhof (connections with the western part of Austria, West Germany, Switzerland), the Südbahnhof (for links with southern Austria, Hungary, Yugoslavia and Italy) and the Franz-Josefs-Bahnhof (connections with north and northwest Austria, Czechoslovakia).

T   Tickets can be purchased and reservations made in travel agencies or at the railway stations. There are reductions available such as the "Austria Ticket" or the "Junior Austria Ticket", and children under six travel free. For all train information, telephone number 72 00. Following is a description of the types of trains found in Austria:

Expresszug *Schnellzug*	1st and 2nd class, the fastest trains
Städteschnellzug	The biggest towns in Austria are connected by these very fast, convenient trains, which leave Vienna every two hours from 7 a.m.
Eilzug	1st and 2nd class; make a number of local stops
Personenzug	local trains which stop at almost every station

Schlafwagen Sleeping car with 1-, 2- or 3-bed compartments including washing facilities.	*Speisewagen* Dining-car	*Liegewagen* Sleeping-berth car (couchette) with blankets, sheets and pillows.

When's the best/next train to…?	**Wann fährt der günstigste/ nächste Zug nach…?**
single (one-way)	**einfach**
return (round-trip)	**hin und zurück**
first/second class	**erste/zweite Klasse**
I'd like to make a seat reservation.	**Ich möchte einen Platz reservieren.**

W   **WATER** *(Wasser).* Viennese water, which comes from the Styrian Alps, tastes mountain-fresh, so for the time being the Viennese don't have to worry about making a distinction between tap water and drinking water. If you come across a sign *Kein Trinkwasser,* however, the water is not fit for drinking.

YOUTH HOSTELS *(Jugendherberge).* If you are planning to make extensive use of youth hostels during your stay in Austria, contact your national youth hostel association before departure to obtain an international membership card. Information about youth hostels in Austria can be obtained through:

Austrian Youth Hostels Association, Gonzagagasse 22, 1010 Vienna.

SOME USEFUL EXPRESSIONS

yes/no	**ja/nein**
please/thank you	**bitte/danke**
excuse me/you're welcome	**Entschuldigung/gern geschehen**
how long/how far	**wie lange/wie weit**
where/when/how	**wo/wann/wie**
yesterday/today/tomorrow	**gestern/heute/morgen**
day/week/month/year	**Tag/Woche/Monat/Jahr**
left/right	**links/rechts**
big/small	**gross/klein**
cheap/expensive	**billig/teuer**
open/closed	**offen/geschlossen**
hot/cold	**heiss/kalt**
old/new	**alt/neu**
I don't understand.	**Ich verstehe nicht.**
Please write it down.	**Schreiben Sie es bitte auf.**
What does this mean?	**Was heisst das?**
I'd like…	**Ich hätte gern…**
How much is that?	**Wieviel kostet das?**
Please help me.	**Bitte helfen Sie mir.**
Fetch a doctor—quickly!	**Holen Sie einen Arzt – schnell!**
Waiter/waitress (please).	**Herr Ober/Fräulein (bitte).**

Index

An asterisk (*) next to a page number indicates a map reference.

INDEX